CABINET GOVERNMENT
AND WAR

THE
LEES KNOWLES LECTURES
1957

1

CABINET
GOVERNMENT
AND WAR
1890-1940

BY

JOHN EHRMAN
Sometime Fellow of Trinity College
Cambridge

ARCHON BOOKS
1969

FIRST PUBLISHED 1958
REPRINTED 1969 WITH PERMISSION OF
THE CAMBRIDGE UNIVERSITY PRESS
IN AN UNALTERED AND UNABRIDGED EDITION

SBN: 208 00737 7
LIBRARY OF CONGRESS CATALOG CARD NUMBER: 69-15790
PRINTED IN THE UNITED STATES OF AMERICA

CONTENTS

PREFACE

THIS book comprises the Lees Knowles lectures delivered at Cambridge in 1957; and I must express my deep gratitude to the Master and Fellows of Trinity for inviting me to give them. It represents an attempt to consider one aspect of recent constitutional history as a whole. For the development of a national system of defence in this century has been of great importance not only to the conduct of war but also to the conduct of government, in an age in which war has played so prominent a part. And while the former process has been examined on various occasions, and in some detail, the latter has not been looked at so closely for its effect on an historical constitutional tradition.

Yet that effect has been significant. The two World Wars are prominent among the factors responsible for transforming the range and nature of British government over the past fifty years—at the least, they have set the pace and the exact form of a development that otherwise might have come about differently. The problems and conditions may often have been remote from those of peace; the experience gained, and the methods adopted, irrelevant to peacetime needs. But the machinery of administration, and administration itself, appear differently as a result. At the close of the nineteenth century, the system of central government could virtually ignore the demands of war, and was still not attuned in many respects to the implications of an industrial society. It has since had to take the former fully into account, and in ways which have helped to shape its treatment of the latter. Governments have found, under pressure of war, that in trying to control one set of problems they have been led inexorably to control others, until almost every aspect of the national life has been acknowledged as subject to supervision. Before 1914, Sir Frederick Maurice once observed, the idea of 'a nation in arms', in the sense in which European nations applied it to their armed forces, had little meaning in this country. 'We know now that it comprises much more than the men who bear arms.'[1]

But at the same time, these great changes have not done violence to the traditional pattern of authority. Alone of the major Powers that have endured the full course of both World Wars, Britain has survived without destroying or devitalizing her familiar institutions. Various reasons may be adduced, some lying beyond the strict confines of government: the resilience of the economy, the response of the Parliamentary system to a remarkably united national sentiment, the character of the British people. But the extent to which such conditions have been free to operate has depended on the activities of government itself; and the survival of the traditional structure has been due largely to the fact that it was already being developed to meet new needs of defence before the First World War, and in ways which enabled it to be adjusted later to unforeseeable and unprecedented strains. As a result, Cabinet government today, after all the intervening developments, retains its

[1] Major-General Sir Frederick Maurice, *Governments and War* (1926), p. 124.

fundamental characteristics and its accustomed strength. The military power remains subordinate to the civil, and the civil power has not suffered a drastic change of form. Sir Winston Churchill, for instance, would no doubt see many differences between the instrument over which he presided in the 1950's and that which he joined in 1908. But it remains essentially the same instrument.

The story, therefore, is one of change combined with continuity—of change, on a scale not before experienced within a comparable period, brought about within, and by means of, a traditional pattern of authority. The principal agent in this process has been a central Committee system, which first brought new developments in the Service Staffs into relation with the Cabinet, and thereafter linked them, and the Cabinet itself, with the extended range of Departmental administration. In its later stages, this central organization has presented a formidable hierarchy of its own. But at first, and indeed for a considerable time, it was small and in some respects informal; and it revolved a good deal—even more than government at the centre normally revolves—around the contributions and the interplay of personalities. It is always possible to exaggerate the importance of such a factor. But it can also easily be underrated in a study of constitutional change; and since we are largely concerned in these lectures with the movements of impersonal bodies, it is as well to remind ourselves here that they have centred on a highly personal world.

In following these movements, I have not attempted to describe in detail all the developments to the machinery. Much may be found in the standard works on the

Cabinet and central government—notably in those by Keith and Sir Ivor Jennings, and in a recent survey from the Royal Institute of Public Administration—in histories sponsored or approved by the Government, in Lord Hankey's books, and in articles in journals, particularly the *Journal of the Royal United Service Institution*, *The Political Quarterly*, and *Public Administration*. To enter regularly into detail, moreover, would have meant devoting more space to the later than to the earlier years. But since, on the contrary, it is the latter which have seemed to me most important to an understanding of the process, I have preferred to lay the emphasis on the earlier part of the period, culminating in the seminal years 1916–18.

I have carried the story to 1940: a date which perhaps may seem surprising at first sight. The reasons are given briefly in the first lecture; but I would like to enlarge on them slightly here. To have continued to 1945, as might perhaps have seemed more natural, would have meant examining in some detail the effects of the changes to the central organization that were introduced in 1940 and 1941; and this is impossible to do satisfactorily without evidence which we await from the official histories on grand strategy for 1941–43. The middle years of the Second World War were important for administration, and it would be unwise to try to appraise them in advance of the authoritative military accounts. But 1940 in any case marks the beginning of a new phase at which we may well pause, to see the position which confronted the new Government, the motives which led to its fresh developments, and the factors which determined its freedom of choice. We are still involved in the results of those last extensive changes, and it is perhaps wise to stop at the point where they were about to be introduced.

Lack of evidence is not, of course, confined to the years since 1940. The published sources covering the half-century to that date do not give all the information one would wish, particularly for the period between the two World Wars. But they give a great deal, and I think more than is often supposed. The material is widely scattered—in official histories of Governments and institutions, in Command Papers, Parliamentary Debates, memoirs and biographies, addresses, lectures and articles —and I have accordingly confined my notes, in a brief text, to direct quotations and to a few specific points. I have had the great good fortune, in trying to interpret the evidence, to receive help and criticism from Lord Hankey, Sir Norman Brook and Professor N. H. Gibbs, all of whom I would thank most warmly for their kindness in allowing me to consult their great knowledge and experience of these matters, and for the trouble they have taken in reading the text despite their many commitments. But it is notoriously a hazardous business to try to trace a pattern in recent events; and the customary author's apology, that he alone is responsible for the defects in his work, applies here with special force. These lectures were written in the hope that they might lead more people to consider the questions. If their publication helps to do so, it will have served its purpose.

J. E.

LONDON
July, 1957

CHAPTER I

THE ORIGINS OF A SYSTEM

FASHIONS in lectures presumably reflect to some extent the movement of historical interest; and it is not surprising that, in the series of Lees Knowles lectures, each of the two World Wars should have been followed by a renewed attention to the problems of the higher strategic organization. Two such occasions stand out: Sir Frederick Maurice's lectures in 1926 on 'Governments and War', and Lord Hankey's in 1945 on 'Government Control in War'. Although the historical material was somewhat different in each case, these two series had certain features in common. Both were founded on personal experience of the subject—Lord Hankey's on unique experience—the purpose in both was partly didactic, and the themes were in part historical and in part prophetic.

The lectures which I have the honour to give cannot follow a similar course. My knowledge of the subject, such as it is, derives purely from academic study; nor am I qualified to envisage the future. I would like rather to examine, on historical lines and as a single historical problem, the development of British Governments' organization for war over a period of some fifty years, from the years around 1890 to 1940.

This organization has centred on the Cabinet; and it is as an aspect of Cabinet government that I want primarily to examine it. But that does not mean to say we should be confined to studying the Cabinet alone, or to a formal and legalistic review of its institutions. On the contrary, developments in the central system can be explained only by reference to those in other fields of government, and against the background of the circumstances to which government responds. Cabinet control rests on administration by Departments, and, in the field of defence, on advice from the Service Staffs. The relations between the three elements must be followed continuously, in the light of the forces responsible for change.

What were those forces? And do they make of the years I have chosen a period that can be studied as a whole? It may perhaps be argued that they do not. In the first place, my terminal year of 1940 is obviously terminal only for these lectures. It looks forward itself to 1945; and I have stopped at the earlier date because we await an authoritative account of the whole period of Mr Churchill's Administration, and because I think there are certain advantages in showing, perhaps more clearly by this means, the nature of the legacy it inherited and on which in turn it built. But if we take the larger span, from the years around 1890 to 1945, it may still perhaps be argued that it does not form an historical period. It could be claimed that decisive developments took place at different points within those years: that, for instance, one era of warfare ended, and another began, in 1915–16, or that the attitude of the British people to war changed fundamentally between 1918 and 1936. It might also be argued that to relate problems so closely to periods is to disregard a warning long since delivered in this University. But in studies relating to war, problems and periods are in fact indivisible; and while it would be rash indeed to try to define this particular period of warfare too closely in all of its aspects, I would suggest that, for our purposes, it is marked by certain features which combine to give it a flavour of its own.

Those features may be sketched very briefly. In the first place, the main enemy, as envisaged from early in the century and as met in two World Wars, was Germany —a fact which involved the greatest shift of strategic emphasis for over two hundred years, and one whose consequences would now seem to be complete. The wars themselves, moreover, were on a scale and of a type never before experienced, and bearing far-reaching results for society and for government. Warfare, which for most of the nineteenth century had remained virtually static in a changing world, was now itself affected by the results of the technological revolution, and was again coming to demand—as it had done earlier, but not in recent decades—a considerable proportion of the nation's financial and economic strength. At the same time, the new weapons, though of unexampled destructiveness and expense, did not prove decisive when the initial attack had been survived. Highly industrialized nations, capable of powerful central control, were thus involved in long and massive struggles, affecting increasingly the whole of the national life. And while the results for society and for government may be carried farther if wars continue, the great process of change itself has taken place, on a scale and with a rapidity which gives it a distinctive character.

Such a process affected, in differing degrees, all of the

belligerents. It found this country better fitted than most to endure its course. At the beginning of the period, Britain was the leading industrial and financial power in the world; and after that supremacy had disappeared, she continued until the later years of the Second World War to increase her production for military purposes. Only then were the limits to the effort revealed, and with them a positive as well as relative decline in a particular system of power and wealth. The traditional strength of that system, moreover, was reflected in and supported by Britain's international position. Despite the growth of the great Dominions, and despite the early lead of France in the First World War and the rise of the United States in the Second, she remained in wartime pre-eminent in the Commonwealth and equal within the Alliances: a state of affairs which would almost certainly not recur in a world war, and might not recur in a period of 'marginal' war.

It is, therefore, perhaps permissible to argue that certain strategic, technological, economic and political conditions have combined to form a period of warfare for this country with marked characteristics of its own. That period in turn produced certain results for government. In this country, it saw the emergence at the centre of a highly articulated Committee system. Indeed, to the student of government we appear in many respects to be living again in a conciliar age: only on this occasion we are governed, over a wide area, not through a Privy Council combining in itself policy and execution, but through a system of Cabinet committees co-ordinating the executive functions of Departments. As the Depart-

4

ments in fact arose upon the foundation of committees of the Council, so the Cabinet committees have been called into existence by the growing multiplicity and range of the Departments. And it is the needs of defence and war which, primarily and directly, have been responsible for this process.

The results, moreover, have been adopted internationally. This is in some ways a surprising development, for in the last quarter of the nineteenth century, when new conditions for war were being formed and fresh thought given to problems of organization, the model most generally admired was the very different Prussian model. But its inelasticity even for the kind of land war originally envisaged, and its later failure to co-ordinate the military and civil sectors of a national effort, became increasingly plain; and it was the British model, developed to suit a maritime and imperial power, that gradually came to be adopted in the Western Alliances for purposes of war, and as a system of linking the needs of defence with a peacetime economy.

This second, international development has its own distinct history; and I shall not attempt to consider it, or that of Allied command with which it is associated, except in so far as they have affected the development of the domestic system. In this first lecture, I propose to discuss the origins from which a fresh organization for defence was formed in this country in the early years of the century; in the second, the growth of that organization to 1914, and its test in the first year and a quarter of war; in the third, its modification and extension from 1916 to 1918; in the last, its subsequent development through a period of quiescence followed by rearmament, and its response to the problems raised by the opening phase of the Second World War.

The starting point for the modern system of a central control of defence is generally taken to be the first report of the Hartington Commission, made in 1889. That body suggested, in the course of its findings, 'the formation of a Naval and Military Council, which should probably be presided over by the Prime Minister, and consist of the Parliamentary Heads of the two services and their principal professional advisers'.[1] This single proposal undoubtedly represented a new departure from familiar practice; and its significance was later confirmed in the form adopted by the Committee of Imperial Defence early in this century. Nevertheless, we must not attribute to the Hartington Commission, at the time it reported, a weight of interest it did not possess. The suggestion, and the review which led up to it, occupied little space in the total of the Commission's reports; and the theoretical and tentative manner in which it was advanced was not indeed calculated to ensure an immediate result.

This was hardly surprising; for the Hartington Commission had not in fact been set up to consider the merits of a co-ordinating council for defence, but to examine the workings of the Admiralty and the War Office and their relations with the Treasury. And as such, it was merely the latest of a long series of investigating bodies which, particularly on the military side, had been brought into being over the past twenty-five years for similar purposes.

[1] Cmd. 5979 (1890), p. viii.

From the later sixties to 1880, no fewer than seventeen Royal Commissions, eighteen Select Committees, nineteen Committees of officers inside the War Office, and thirty-five Committees of Military Officers had considered matters of policy affecting the army. The Commission of 1887 to 1890 was thus the latest example of a practice which had been thoroughly familiar since the reforming decade following the Crimean War.

This is a fact of more than incidental interest. It illustrates an important development which preceded, and accompanied in its early stages, the emergence of a system of Cabinet committees for defence. The movement, in fact, was at first a Departmental movement: a process which, on consideration, is obvious enough. The later nineteenth century was the great age of Departmental government; relations on the official level were defined, in so far as was necessary, by the Treasury; and the Cabinet itself was, to use a phrase of Lord Morley's, 'an assemblage of departmental ministers'.[1] As the co-ordinating committees began to take root, it was therefore as emanations of a parent system to which they contributed specific services on specific occasions, and on whose direct support they depended entirely. It was indeed a feature of their existence almost to the eve of the First World War that where a committee, however powerful its constitution, failed to attract the interest of a Department intimately concerned, it invariably languished or was ineffectual.

To many reformers, therefore—to Wolseley, for instance, at the War Office, and later to Fisher at the

[1] John Morley, *The Life of William Ewart Gladstone*, vol. II (1903), p. 414.

Admiralty—the administrative problems were of the familiar kind. But two great developments were in fact under way which combined to transform, instead of as previously to modify, the existing organization. First, questions of defence were affected increasingly by developments within the Empire. The latter were indeed responsible chronologically for the earliest steps towards co-ordination, and helped to mould the later system in important respects. When the reforming spirit of the sixties had turned to Imperial concerns, it had been to ensure economy and a minimum of interference with the territories overseas. The emphasis, for defence, had therefore been on Colonial self-help, and the motives governing the policy endured in powerful elements of both political parties. But as the expansionist activities of the seventies bore fruit, particularly in Africa, the policy itself had increasingly to be adjusted to the consequences in the self-governing Colonies. In the middle eighties, Colonial land forces began in their turn to be involved on a small scale in Imperial operations overseas, while a major reorganization in India, undertaken for different purposes in the second half of the decade, made the forces of the sub-continent more readily available for service elsewhere. In a space of fifteen years they took part in seven campaigns abroad, and were used increasingly as garrisons overseas. By the time of the South African War, Colonial and Indian military help was thus familiar in principle and no longer negligible in extent.

In these conditions, not even Gladstonian Administrations could ignore entirely proposals from Colonial Governments on matters of defence. As the Colonial

Secretary, Lord Carnarvon, wrote to *The Times* of the Australians in 1888,[1] 'with smaller means they have shown an appreciation of the risks of modern war and of the requirements of modern defence, which English Governments have been slow to understand'. London's response, indeed, was for long in a minor key. The beginnings, as Professor Gibbs has recently shown,[2] may be traced to March 1878, when one of the recurrent scares of war with Russia arose in the course of the Russo-Turkish War. A small 'inner Cabinet' was then watching events and directing action. At a lower level, the Colonial Office decided to form a small Colonial Defence Committee, consisting of one of its own officials with a representative of the Admiralty and of the War Office, to consider the defence of certain Colonial ports in the event of war. This *ad hoc* body soon disappeared, when the tension died down; and its sequel, so far from being a more powerful and permanent Government committee, as two of its members had recommended, was the more familiar expedient of a Royal Commission, 'on the Defence of British Possessions and Commerce Abroad', which soon found itself confined to considering the defence of naval coaling stations. But the very inadequacy of this Commission led, within a few years, to a more significant step. For in 1885, when the possibility again arose of trouble with Russia, a new Colonial Defence Committee was set up, empowered to consider representations from the Colonies on those matters affect-

---

[1] *The Times*, 9 July 1888; cited in Sir Charles Lucas, *The Empire at War*, vol. I (1921), p. 142.
[2] N. H. Gibbs, *The Origins of Imperial Defence* (1955), p. 9.

ing their defences for which the terms of the Royal Commission did not provide. As earlier, the Committee consisted initially of representatives of the Colonial Office itself and of the two Service Departments, with an official from the Treasury added later. It took over the secretary of the Royal Commission, who was soon succeeded by Captain George Sydenham Clarke, later Lord Sydenham of Combe and the first in that line of expert secretaries to committees of defence who in due course were to leave a mark on British constitutional practice. This Committee lasted, without interruption, until it was incorporated as a sub-Committee in the later structure of Imperial defence.

The Committee worked hard, and with some success. Taking within its scope all Colonies except the four 'fortresses' of Gibraltar, Malta, Bermuda and Halifax, in its first three and a half years it reviewed sixty-one local schemes of defence, made detailed proposals for the strengths of all Colonial garrisons, and in addition, according to its secretary, 'dealt with 151 subjects of the most varied character, almost all of our recommendations being accepted and acted upon'.[1] This was something new, and of distinct value. The Committee contained at different times some exceptionally able men, who later were to rise to high position; it was active and well informed; and, within its limits, was able to affect the way in which problems of defence were studied. But those limits were real, if ill defined. The Committee's status was junior, its members being officials, not of high seniority; it was confined to recommen-

[1] Colonel Lord Sydenham of Combe, *My Working Life* (1927), p. 72.

dation, and in theory on the initiative of the Colonies; and its relations with higher authority in London seem to have been nebulous. Its superior in the first few years was, apparently, a Colonial Committee of the Cabinet. But, in common no doubt with other Cabinet committees now vanished, it left no records, we know nothing of its work, and, from the fact that it accepted almost all of the recommendations submitted to it, either was not very active or did not consider the work of its subordinate to be of great importance. We are left with the impression, in the field of Imperial defence at this time, of an energetic subordinate body, interesting itself in the subject as widely as it dared and as its resources allowed, but limited in its capacity and, as its secretary has admitted, becoming unpopular in Whitehall when it ventured to extend its scope.

The Committee's investigations proved of some use to the Governments assembled at the first Colonial Conference, in 1887: the more so, as that Conference was concerned primarily with questions of defence. But those questions were themselves embryonic, and there was little consensus of opinion on them. The attitude of the British Government was cautious. As Lord Salisbury took pains to warn his audience, in opening the proceedings, they must be 'prosaic', and indeed to one irritated Australian delegate the speech 'might have been made by a French Minister'. Nor were the Colonies in a position to press for ambitious schemes. A growing sense of their own identities restrained some of them in any case from wishing to do so; and, among the greater number who did so wish, strategic doctrines were still too unformed for any coherent pressure to emerge from the cross-currents of local interests and enthusiasms. In naval affairs, for instance, the traditional British conception of a unified and flexible strategy encountered tendencies towards a purely local self-defence on the part of those Australasian Colonies whose proposals for military association with Britain went beyond those of the home country herself. The results of the Conference accordingly were limited. Nor, despite the pride of Empire displayed at the Diamond Jubilee of 1897, were matters advanced farther at the next Conference in that year. It remained for the South African War to stimulate the development of an Imperial, as of a British, organization. By the time that the Colonial Conference of 1902 assembled, the subject had become one of prominence, and new ideas were arising in London as well as in some of the territories overseas. The most extreme suggestion, indeed, now came from the War Office, in a memorandum proposing a scheme of close co-ordination, with definite commitments, for the land forces throughout the Empire. This was submitted to the Conference; and its fate was instructive. Despite the support of some of the Colonies, Canada and, more surprisingly, Australia combined to defeat the proposal, and to pass a resolution in its place approving 'defence schemes in co-operation with the Imperial Government and under the advice of Imperial officers, but only so far as was consistent with the prospects of local self-government'.[1]

Closer co-ordination was achieved in the naval sphere, with the Australasian and African governments. But

[1] Lucas, loc. cit. p. 152.

here again Canada held aloof; and the distinguishing feature of the Conference was indeed the way in which the Canadian Government's concern for its independent rights served to focus similar concerns on the part of the other Colonies, at different times and on different issues. This proved to be of great importance. For at a time when the prospect of a more effective central control had been given a powerful stimulus, and when the Home Government was seeking its way, for the first time, towards a closer integration of the land as of the sea forces, the process was directed into different channels by the Colonies themselves. And when, at the end of 1902, Balfour's Government created the Committee of Imperial Defence, the insistence which was then laid on its consultative and advisory capacities was acknowledged to be in part the result of the recent Conference. As Balfour himself remarked on more than one occasion, this emphasis made of the Committee 'a truly Imperial body', capable, by its very restriction to precept and advice, of harmonizing the separate interests and aspirations of countries responsible, at least in certain aspects, for their own affairs.

The evolution of the self-governing Colonies, which had fostered the earliest, limited movement in this country towards co-ordination in matters of defence, thus helped to mould the nature, as it decided the title, of the later, more elaborate system. But that system was not brought into existence directly by Imperial developments. It was rather the immediate product of purely British needs, which by the end of the South African War had become urgent and undisguised.

For it was the South African War that brought to a point the dissatisfaction which the reformers in and beyond the Services, and particularly those concerned with the army, had felt keenly for many years. The fact that the war was a land war, and that the navy at the time was at the crest of one of its recurrent curves of efficiency, concentrated attention on the War Office; and it was around that unfortunate institution that more Royal Commissions and Select Committees gathered. For the weaknesses of the army were primarily weaknesses of the War Office. In many respects, indeed, British military reputation was high in the two decades before the South African War. The succession of Colonial campaigns had bred an art in their management, and a group of commanders, respected throughout Europe and forming a distinctive element of British power and prestige. Nor was all entirely black at the War Office itself. Between 1885 and 1890—the period of Wolseley's tenure as Quartermaster-General—there had been a marked advance in many administrative fields, and a small group of officers had begun to think afresh about the problems of the army and of national defence. The fruits of some of these activities were indeed to be seen early in the South African War. The small Intelligence Division—despite the accusations levelled at it later—gave accurate warning of the Boers' position on the eve; the Mobilization Division assembled the forces ordered with notable speed and efficiency; the arrangements for supply on a growing scale and over a long line of communications were in general satisfactory; and the manner in which the forces recovered from their early discomfitures at least argued a flexibility which at the time would not necessarily have been paralleled in all of the larger European armies. But the later tactical and strategic achievements were the achievements of the men on the spot; and it was significant that those of the War Office should have been almost entirely administrative. As a policy-making body, it was indeed lamentably weak. It failed completely to gauge the nature of the war, its instructions and information to the early commanders were meagre and vague, and the composition, organization and training of the forces and Staffs initially sent out reflected an utter misdirection, where they did not reveal an absence, of strategic and tactical thought. The strength of the vital Railway Staff, for instance, for an area as large as central Europe, seems to have been settled at first as one officer, one batman, one horse and one groom.[1] It was not to be wondered at, when such things came to light, that Joseph Chamberlain should have feared the War Office more than the Boers.

The relative competence of the Intelligence and Mobilization Divisions pointed the moral to this unhappy tale. For they formed the only elements of a General Staff in the War Office, being indeed the last survivors of that virtually forgotten part of the Quartermaster-General's department which had served the army in such a capacity at least from the days of Marlborough to those of Wellington. And while this lack of a central Staff had not seriously affected the conduct of the small and isolated

[1] According to the D.A.A.G. on the Headquarters' Staff responsible for railways. See Lieutenant-Colonel Charles à Court Repington, *Vestigia* (1919), p. 207.

Colonial expeditions, it was another matter when the latest of the series was revealed as a large-scale war, making substantial demands on the resources of the country.

For such a war, the higher organization of the War Office remained almost entirely unfit. There had been a number of changes since the great War Office Act of 1870; but the conditions of warfare and the background to the changes themselves had rendered the results virtually negligible. In the later nineteenth century in Europe, the reappearance of larger armies, now at the disposal of more easily informed central authorities, had led to fresh thought on the relations between the centre and the Commands, and on the overriding need for a higher standard of Staff work. But land wars for this country were still Colonial or Indian wars; while the burden of thought within the War Office itself had lain since 1870 on the relations between the Secretary of State and the Commander-in-Chief, a constitutional problem to which all subsidiary questions of organization ultimately referred, and which cut across, and confused, any proper devolution of powers from the centre and any proper distinction between administration and policy. The elements of reform in the army thus remained elements, combined into no coherent scheme, while the changes to the system at the centre merely reflected the tangle which had given them birth.

The remedy was seen, and lost sight of, in the late eighties and early nineties. The Act of 1870 had left intact various of the self-governing authorities in the War Office, who came under a common control only on reaching the Secretary of State himself. But throughout the eighties the Commander-in-Chief, the senior of those authorities, the commander of the home forces, and responsible directly to the Sovereign as well as to the Secretary of State, steadily increased his powers over the rest. The climax came in 1888, when he was placed directly in charge of a range of administrative and operational Departments which gave him greater powers than any of his predecessors since Monck. But the reaction was already under way. When the Hartington Commission reported finally in 1890, it recommended that the office of Commander-in-Chief should be abolished, and that his administrative responsibilities should be given to a number of departments, whose heads should form a War Office Council with the Secretary of State, his powers of command to a General commanding the home forces, and his responsibility for advice to a Chief of Staff to the Secretary of State. Here, it may seem in retrospect, was the chance that should not have been missed. But the disappearance of the Commander-in-Chief was a revolutionary proposal, startling even many of the reformers; and in the event a different solution was adopted. It is significant that it should have turned on the introduction of a Chief of Staff. For while the changes in administration and command were readily accepted, the Secretary of State, Campbell-Bannerman, shrank from creating a General Staff in a country in which he conceived there was 'no room for "general military policy" in this larger and more ambitious sense of the phrase', and where a body devoted entirely to planning for war might accordingly prove 'some danger to our best interests'.[1] Preferring therefore to retain the traditional form of professional advice, he proposed to place the Commander-in-Chief at the head of a new Army Board, composed of the heads of the military departments and itself forming part of a new Consultative Council to the Secretary of State. This blueprint was adopted, virtually in its entirety, in 1895.

The change brought some advantages to administration, and confirmed the constitutional supremacy of the Minister over his principal professional adviser. But as a system of authority and for deciding policy, it proved a useless compromise. The Commander-in-Chief soon found himself—as Wolseley, the new incumbent of that office, put it, in words which were to find a curious echo over forty years later—'the fifth wheel of the coach';[2] the relations between him, the Council and the Board were never satisfactorily settled; the War Office continued to engross matters better left to the Commands; and the formation of a General Staff was summarily prevented. The latest development of the machinery was thus to prove irrelevant to the problems it had soon to meet.

In both the public and official minds in the nineties, a complete contrast to the administration of the army was provided by that of the navy. The relations between the First Lord and his professional advisers, regulated under the Admiralty Patent by Orders in Council of 1872 and 1882, had settled on an amicable basis, and a recent reorganization of the Fleet, centering on the Naval Defence

[1] J. A. Spender, *The Life of the Right Hon. Sir Henry Campbell-Bannerman, G.C.B.*, vol. 1 (1923), p. 118.

[2] Major-General Sir F. Maurice and Sir George Arthur, *The Life of Lord Wolseley* (1924), p. 295.

Act of 1889, satisfied the country that the Department was efficient. At the turn of the century, the navy stood very high in the nation's affections and esteem; and it was not surprising that the model for the reform of the War Office, proposed by investigating bodies from 1890 to 1904, should have been the Board of Admiralty.

The Board's achievements, it was true, had been considerable since the later eighties. At that time, the Fleet had sunk to what has been described as 'the lowest level of efficiency of material that the British Navy had known since the middle of the eighteenth century'.[1] The rapid advances in design, in propulsion and in armament made fashions in building ships, as Mr Gladstone observed, 'as fickle as that of ladies' hats'; and the consequences for administration, as revealed by the Russian crisis of 1885, proved temporarily disastrous. Manœuvres (first held on that occasion), gunnery, organization in the Fleet and in the dockyards, all disclosed grave defects; while the Admiralty itself was, to quote the First Lord of the day, 'in a state of administrative chaos'.[2] Twelve years later, at the Diamond Jubilee review, a balanced and modernized Fleet stretched, in its squadrons, for over thirty miles; and the array had been assembled without calling on a single foreign station. The material and organization which lay behind it had been entirely overhauled; and the traditional naval supremacy of Britain was again universally acknowledged.

More great reforms were soon to follow, in the first

[1] Admiral Sir Reginald H. Bacon, *A Naval Scrap-Book* (1925), pp. 155–6.
[2] Lord George Hamilton, *Parliamentary Reminiscences and Reflections, 1868 to 1885* (1916), p. 278.

2-2

decade of the new century. But this vigour in administration concealed weaknesses, as yet scarcely recognized, within the Admiralty as a body for determining policy. There was no provision, either in the career of the naval officer or within the Department, for instruction or thought on matters of strategy. An embryonic Staff work was beginning to emerge from the Fleet manœuvres instituted regularly in the nineties, and a few advanced minds, such as Fisher's, saw the need for 'a big *thinking* Department'. But that Department failed to appear, not least under Fisher's later administration; there was no Naval Staff at the Admiralty, as there was no General Staff at the War Office; and the ready response of the naval administration to the continuing challenges of new material was accompanied by a curiously static and complacent attitude to the strategic problems of war.

At the turn of the century, therefore, the main problem of national defence appeared to be a Staff problem—the creation in each of the Service Departments of a thinking organ, and the realignment of those Departments so far as was necessary to relate the new organ to the direction of policy. But the introduction of such a system must be influenced by considerations outside the competence of the Service Departments themselves. For how could such Departments think to any good purpose in the absence of a national strategy? The two problems, in fact, were complementary, as the course of events over the next decade was to show. No national strategy was possible without a reorganization in the Departments; but reorganization in a Department would not of itself meet the case, without a more effective co-operation between the Services and a proper connexion between them and a central organ of national strategy.

The emphasis at this point, in fact, rested to a greater degree than usual on a change of machinery. Such changes are sometimes taken as in themselves solutions to strategic problems. Obviously, this is far from always being so. The effect of any system of control depends on, even as it influences, other factors, most of which are the direct concern of other agencies: on the provision, for instance, of the right material, in the hands of the right men; on education, training and morale in the forces; on political harmony, and on economic strength. But at the time of which we are speaking, the importance of a reform in organization lay precisely in the fact that all of these other activities depended upon it for their own development. Improvements in the Services, of whatever type—of material and administration, as well as of policy—were now confused and retarded by the confusion or lack of a system for strategic thought. The various groups of reformers, however different their solutions, were right in agreeing on the urgent need for reform.

The close interaction of the two processes—reform within the Departments, and the provision of a central control—was illustrated towards the close of the century both by the variety of the remedies proposed and by the failure of the expedients adopted. The confusion between the two levels of authority involved could be seen in Wolseley's remark, when Commander-in-Chief of the Army, on the Hartington Commission and its sequel in the War Office: 'I thought in my foolishness that the

Hartington Commission was going, at least, to give us the means of making real plans of campaign with statesmen, soldiers, and sailors all working together, and the only use they have made of it is to clip my wings.'[1] The failure to resolve what were two separate problems, precisely by constructing a proper relationship between them, was in fact producing impractical suggestions in theory and ineffectual results in practice. This was the period of proposals for the resuscitation of a Lord High Admiral and a Commander-in-Chief with supreme powers; it was also the period of the controversy over 'the single responsible adviser', a conception advanced by Sir Charles Dilke and developed principally by Spenser Wilkinson. But if some of the proposals envisaged a solution outside or parallel to the normal Ministerial system, it was because that system seemed unable to adapt itself to the demands. The recommendation of the Hartington Commission, for a Council of Defence probably under the Prime Minister, had not been followed. Instead, in 1891 a more modest expedient had been adopted, of a more familiar nature—a joint Naval and Military Committee of Defence, appointed by the Secretary of State for War, responsible at first to the War Office and later to the War Office and the Admiralty, consisting of six professional members under the presidency of the Parliamentary Under-Secretary of State for War, and charged with considering matters of policy affecting the coastal defences of interest to both Departments. This Committee proved to be of little importance. It helped, in some slight measure, to bring the Services together on specific

[1] Maurice and Arthur, *Life of Lord Wolseley*, p. 286.

22

issues; and its methods of business, with their provision for agenda and minutes, circulation of papers to executive bodies, and a division of duties between a naval and a military secretary, gave an interesting foretaste of the arrangements of the Committee of Imperial Defence. But in its status, its limits, and its subordination to a Department, the new Committee, despite its impressive title, resembled the Colonial Defence Committee of 1885 —with which, and in some respects over which, it was enjoined to act—rather than that superior co-ordinating body which the Hartington Commission had envisaged.

The need for such a body was indeed neither increased nor reduced by the creation of the Joint Naval and Military Committee; and, towards the end of 1894, Ministers seem to have recognized the fact. In the following year, the Prime Minister, Lord Salisbury, invited the Lord President of the Council, the Duke of Devonshire—the Hartington of the Hartington Commission—to preside over a standing Defence Committee of the Cabinet, empowered to examine questions of defence in general. This Committee lasted until 1902, its members, at least at the turn of the century, being the Lord President of the Council, the First Lord of the Treasury (the Prime Minister being in the Lords), the Chancellor of the Exchequer, the First Lord of the Admiralty and the Secretary of State for War.

But, despite its powerful composition, the Defence Committee proved almost entirely ineffective. We know little of its work, for again no records have descended to us. But from the criticisms of the Royal Commission on the South African War, and from the adverse—indeed scathing—Parliamentary and published comments of contemporaries, there would seem to be little to know. The Committee was responsible, in the 'Black Week' of the South African War, for inviting Roberts to take command; but that was an urgent decision which had in fact already been settled by an inner group of Ministers, and in the work for which a standing body was deemed advisable the Committee had little to propose. It seems to have met irregularly and seldom, and when it met to have devoted itself primarily to considering financial questions and to settling specific inter-Departmental disputes. If this was so, however, it was perhaps only natural. With no Staff thought to guide it in considering principles affecting the future, Ministers were perforce confined to dealing, when asked, with the more awkward administrative details of the present. The provision of a Cabinet committee, essential as it was within the framework of a proper system of defence, remained merely a development on paper when that system did not exist.

The Defence Committee accordingly attracted nothing but odium. To the reformers it was, as Arnold-Foster put it, 'a joke and a very bad one';[1] and within the Government too it was recognized as a failure. In the early days of the new century, there was a growing agreement that something must soon be done. From whatever aspect the problems were examined—whether from a Department or from the Cabinet, as a professional issue or as an element of government—the same broad conclusions now emerged. 'We have never', said Wolseley

[1] H. O. Arnold-Foster, *The War Office, The Army and The Empire* (1900), p. 75.

for the army in 1902, 'formulated to ourselves, as a Power, as a People, or as a Government—we had never put on paper to be translated from one Government to another—what were the objects for which our Army was created and maintained.'[1] 'We have been shamefully unbusinesslike', admitted Lord Selborne at the Admiralty in 1903, 'in the way we have treated questions of national defence.'[2] 'I do not believe', observed the Prime Minister in 1900, 'in the perfection of the British Constitution as an instrument for war.'[3] And as an element of government, defence was equally unsatisfactory. Although the percentage of expenditure on the Services within the national budget had not risen appreciably in the decade preceding the South African War, the increase had been considerable in terms of money, and in the rate at which that had taken place. The cost of the armed forces had risen by only $4\frac{1}{2}$ per cent between 1887/8 and 1892/3; but it had risen another 38 per cent by the eve of the South African War, and for the navy alone by over 68 per cent. Such figures alarmed many contemporaries, not least for the power they might confer on the professional elements within the Service Departments. But they were dwarfed by those of the South African War, which cost some £217 million (over double the total national expenditure of any year in the middle nineties) and added over £149 million (over 20 per cent) to the National Debt. Such expenditure, coupled on the one hand with the Jingo spirit and on the other with the

[1] Maurice and Arthur, loc. cit. p. 327.
[2] Arthur J. Marder, *British Naval Policy, 1880–1905* (n.d., but 1941), p. 417.
[3] *Parliamentary Debates (Fourth Series)*, vol. LXXVIII, col. 30.

results in the war itself, alarmed, for these various reasons, Ministers and sections of the public alike. In 1900, and again in 1902, the Chancellor of the Exchequer, Hicks Beach, publicly criticized the army on the score of value for money. At about the same time, Salisbury was stressing the other side of the picture, in a private letter expatiating on the implications for finance and morality of 'the heads of our defensive departments surrender[ing] themselves to the fatal guidance of their professional advisers'.[1] In the years that followed, the desire to re-establish economy and an adequate Ministerial control accompanied the need for efficiency as inducements to reform in defence.

The threads were drawn together in the three years following the South African War. That short period witnessed the publication of a series of valuable reports on various aspects of defence. In 1901, there appeared Wolseley's memorandum of 1900 to the Prime Minister on the recent changes in the War Office, and the report of the Select Committee of the House of Commons into War Office Organization (the Clinton Dawkins Committee); in the autumn of 1903, the massive report of the Royal Commission on the South African War (the Elgin Commission); in January 1904, the report of the War Office Reconstruction Committee (the Esher Committee); and later in that year, the report of the Royal Commission on the Militia and Volunteers (the Norfolk Commission).[2] This rapid accumulation of detailed and

[1] Lady Victoria Hicks Beach, *Life of Sir Michael Hicks Beach* (*Earl St Aldwyn*), vol. II (1932), p. 153.

[2] Respectively Cmd. 512 (1901); 581 (1901); 1789, 1790, 1791, 1792 (1903); 1932, 1968, 2002 (1904); and 2061 (1904).

weighty evidence increased a public interest already aroused, and enabled answers to be given to many of the questions that were now being freely asked. But that interest and discussion had already been concentrated by the fate of a proposal from the War Office itself. In March 1901, the Secretary of State, St John Brodrick, announced an ambitious plan for the expansion and reorganization of the army in six Army Corps, three to be complete and three in cadre only. The scheme, envisaging an army of some 600,000 men and obviously involving great cost, was at once attacked on every side. The traditional elements of the Liberal Party opposed it on the grounds of morality and expense; the Liberal Imperialists, the Conservative 'Hughligans', and the group of reforming publicists combined to oppose it as inefficient; while the 'blue-water' naval school attacked the whole conception of reliance on large land forces. The scheme, raising as it did a heavier structure on foundations already known to be unsound, was indeed badly thought out and largely unworkable; and it sank without trace amid the ridicule it provoked. But it had served to focus the attacks of the various groups of critics, and to produce for the first time, in 1902 and 1903, a sustained Parliamentary consideration of the problems of defence. The results were impressive. As Asquith remarked at the close of one of the more notable occasions, in February 1903, the speeches had shown 'an almost unprecedented consensus of opinion from both sides of the House...as regards the true lines upon which a well-conceived policy of Imperial defence ought to proceed'; and the debate, he thought, would be 'remembered as a landmark in the history of our administrative policy long after the six Army Corps. . . have vanished into the thin air which is their natural element'.[1]

By the time that these words were spoken, the Government had taken a first step. In November 1902, the two Service Ministers recommended to the new Prime Minister, Balfour, that the Defence Committee of the Cabinet should be superseded by a body better equipped to deal with 'the most difficult and important problems of all, those which are neither purely naval nor purely military, nor purely naval and military combined, but which may be described as naval, military and political'.[2] This proposal found an immediate response. As one of the members of the Defence Committee, Balfour had become increasingly disturbed by its inadequacy and interested in the problems of reform; and after an initial hesitation, he acted with despatch. On 18 December 1902, the new Cabinet committee met for the first time. The Lord President, Devonshire, was again chairman; but Balfour himself attended, together with the two Service Ministers, the First Sea Lord and the Commander-in-Chief, and the Directors of Naval and Military Intelligence. The Committee of Imperial Defence had begun its life.

The connexion of the new Committee with the Prime Minister was thus very close from the start. It was recognized at the time that this must be so. As Arnold-

[1] Quoted in The Rt Hon. L. S. Amery, *My Political Life*, vol. 1 (1953), pp. 200–1.
[2] Blanche E. C. Dugdale, *Arthur James Balfour*, vol. 1 (1936), p. 367.

Foster observed, in one of his tracts published in 1900, the Prime Minister was the only man in the Empire with the power necessary to initiate reform; and Balfour himself remarked that one of the reasons for the defects of the earlier system had been that Salisbury 'never paid any attention to these things'. It is therefore no accident that the Committee of Imperial Defence should be peculiarly Balfour's monument. He was himself well aware of its dependence upon him; he took care to be present at every one of the meetings held during his Premiership; and indeed the main reasons why he stayed in office in the increasingly adverse circumstances of 1905 were to complete the revision of British strategy with the Anglo-Japanese Treaty, and to allow a reasonable breathing space to his new committee, which he feared might otherwise succumb to indifference and misuse on the part of his Liberal successors.

For Balfour had clear ideas on the nature of his instrument. They were first expressed in the arrangements for attendance. The meeting of 18 December had seen Ministers, soldiers and sailors assembled together for the first time on a standing committee of Cabinet. To safeguard this association, membership was settled initially *ex officio*; but a year later, the right to admittance was changed. In the winter of 1903, when Devonshire had left the Cabinet, Balfour took the chair which he and his successors were to occupy until August 1914; and in December he told the Committee, as he had already told the Cabinet, that he intended for the future to have no members *ex officio* other than himself. Instead, the Prime Minister 'would summon to each meeting those persons whom he thought best qualified to advise upon [its] business'. This change might have seemed drastic. It turned the Committee, at one move, from an instrument of the Cabinet into an instrument of the Prime Minister —a development which proved to be not entirely without disadvantage. But it was made for two reasons, both of fundamental importance. First, it was designed to ensure that the new Committee was not hampered, in a sphere of government where the problems were unusually varied and were not confined to this country alone, by the rigidity of a fixed membership or by the conventions attaching to the conduct of business by an organ of Cabinet. If Ministers and professional advisers were to combine effectively, and if representatives of other parts of the Empire were to be admitted without embarrassment, attendance must be on a basis of equality, which in Balfour's view was best secured by invitation.

But secondly, this flexibility helped to point the fact, and to reinforce the impression, that the Committee was confined to study and advice. We have already seen the reasons why this should have been so in Imperial affairs. Others were equally cogent in Whitehall. It was obviously undesirable and impossible to do anything which might appear to weaken the responsibility or power of the Service Departments; and indeed, as the history of the Committee was to show at intervals, the fear that it might develop more than advisory functions existed for many years in elements of the Government and of Parliament. A standing committee of Cabinet, with a powerful and novel fixed membership, might have seemed to threaten traditional methods: a Prime Minister's committee, at which attendance was by invitation, perhaps gave less cause for suspicion or alarm.

As it turned out, that suspicion was later to fasten on an aspect of the Committee which was the direct result of this feature of membership. For the emphasis on flexibility underlined the need—already envisaged from the failure of the traditional methods—for an orderly conduct of business by a permanent secretariat. The continuity, in fact, which was not provided by membership must be found in the work of a staff. This was soon recognized, the more so as such staffs already existed in embryo in the sub-Committees on Colonial and coastal defence, and their procedure had been adopted in part. The necessary stimulus was provided by a recommendation from the Esher Committee in January 1904. The wording is of interest. '. . . We have suggested the creation of a "Department", to use a well-understood term, for the Defence Committee, containing elements of a permanent character, following the well-tried and established precedents of British administration, located in close proximity to the residence of the Prime Minister, and under his exclusive control.'[1] Balfour again acted; and, in May and July, Treasury Minutes established a small staff to the Committee, under a Secretary.

With the provision of its secretariat, the Committee of Imperial Defence entered fully upon its work. But the value of that work depended on the co-operation, and thus on the competence, of the Service Departments; and the simultaneous reorganization of the War Office was a landmark as prominent as the appearance of the Cabinet

[1] Cmd. 1932 (1904), p. 2.

committee itself. All was ready by the beginning of
1904. Reform was now inevitable; and in the previous
autumn, the Government had shown that it meant
business by appointing Arnold-Foster, one of the leading
critics, to be Secretary of State. The publication of the
Esher Committee's report provided a detailed basis for
the changes. Its proposals followed almost exactly those
of the Hartington Commission fourteen years before: the
office of Commander-in-Chief should be abolished, an
Army Council should be formed on the pattern of the
Board of Admiralty, and the Secretary of State should be
furnished with a Chief of Staff. But their reception on
this occasion was very different. In February 1904 the
new Army Council was set up, composed of the Secretary
of State, four Military Members of whom the new Chief
of Staff was the First Member, the Parliamentary and
Permanent Under-Secretaries of State, and the Financial
Secretary. Over the next year and a half it embarked on
a far-ranging scheme of reorganization, affecting most of
the branches of the War Office, and the terms of service,
composition and equipment of the forces. These efforts
on the whole were unsuccessful. The War Office was in a
sensitive mood, after so much undesirable publicity and
particularly after some exceptionally rough handling by
the redoubtable Esher Committee; and the new Secretary of State, already tired and impatient of delay, caused
further offence by his open and reiterated conviction that
he had been called to cleanse an Augean stable. By the
end of 1904, it was indeed clear that he had failed to carry
either his Council or the Cabinet with him in inaugurating a new regime. But while the programme proved

disappointing, the means for its enforcement in other hands had been secured: by the revised system of authority, by a better distribution of business within the Department, and, in the course of 1905, by the institution of a General Staff. For in January of that year, a War Office memorandum was issued providing for such a body; and a few weeks before he left office Arnold-Foster set it in motion, with a scheme of organization which his successor followed. When the Conservative Government fell at the end of 1905, the elements of a new system of defence were thus in existence. It remained to be seen how firmly they had been established, and how adequate they were.

CHAPTER II

THE GROWTH AND TEST OF THE SYSTEM, 1906–15

IN January 1906 there was a General Election, and the new Liberal Government was confirmed in power after an interval of ten and a half years. The effect on the nascent system of defence was generally held to be uncertain. Although the group of Liberal Imperialists was well represented in the Cabinet, both the extent and the direction of its influence were doubtful. The strongest traditions of the party remained peace and retrenchment; and while a more competent organization for defence was acknowledged to serve the latter, its development was suspect for its effect on the former. But in the event the new Government continued, and was indeed obliged to develop, the work of its predecessor, within the Services and in the central machinery of control.

The most pressing reform in 1906 remained that of the army. The recent reorganization in the War Office had provided a sounder basis for a programme; but the programme itself had still to be devised and carried out. Arnold-Foster's scheme, well thought out though it had been and in some respects perhaps superior to that eventually adopted, had failed to carry conviction either with the new Army Council or with the Cabinet; and while his work and his difficulties should not be ignored, it remained possible to say, as Lord Roberts said in the summer of 1905, that 'our armed forces, as a body, are as absolutely unfitted and unprepared for war as they were in 1899–1900'.[1]

It was fortunate that the new Government had, among its ablest members, a man deeply interested in the problems of defence, and on bad enough terms with the Prime Minister at the outset to be denied the office which otherwise he might well have held. Ever since he had published his *Life of Adam Smith* in 1887, in which 'the Free Trade doctrine was restated in a form qualified by recognition of the necessity for paying attention to considerations of defence',[2] Haldane had followed such questions closely. Membership of the Moulton Committee on Explosives in the South African War had quickened his interest; and in February 1905, when he was widely regarded as probably the next Lord Chancellor, he was outlining to the Secretary of the Committee of Imperial Defence his ideas for improvements at the War Office, which 'may form the gauge of the success of the Liberal Government'.[3] The opportunity soon came to test the truth of this unfashionable doctrine. Denied the Lord Chancellorship by Campbell-Bannerman's dislike and distrust, and offered the Home Office instead, Haldane preferred to take the Department which, as the Prime Minister told him, 'nobody will touch with a pole'; and it was indeed with a certain sardonic pleasure that Campbell-Bannerman watched the successful and ambitious lawyer enter on so unpopular a task.

---

[1] *Parliamentary Debates (Fourth Series)*, vol. CXLIX, col. 14.

[2] R. B. Haldane, *An Autobiography* (1929), p. 102.

[3] Major-General Sir Frederick Maurice, *Haldane*, vol. I (1937), p. 139.

Haldane himself had no doubts—he was not of a doubting nature—about his continued success, or how he proposed to achieve it. 'Here', he observed later, 'was an almost virgin field, to be operated on by applying first principles as soon as I had discovered them.'[1] The process at first may have puzzled the soldiers. 'When the Army Council asked me one morning again', Haldane relates of his early days in office, 'for some notion of the Army I had in mind, my answer to them was, "A Hegelian Army".' 'The conversation', he continues, 'then fell off.'[2] But in fact it was a peculiarly appropriate moment for such an approach. For Haldane was fortunate in his time. In the spring of 1905 the Kaiser had made his ill-advised speeches in Tangier; and in the following December and January, on the eve of the Algeciras Conference which that disturbance had provoked, information from Berlin caused a sudden scare of war. It was not indeed an idle threat; and while this was not the first scare of war in the new century—one had arisen with Russia only fourteen months before—it was the first time that Germany had been envisaged openly as the potential enemy. The tension soon eased. But Germany's subsequent behaviour revived a fear which had hitherto been at best intermittent; and Haldane's arrival in office therefore coincided exactly with the emergence of a new strategic situation, which gradually came to be recognized as such.

That situation demanded a reassessment of the various strategic assumptions which had existed, in uneasy and

[1] Haldane, *An Autobiography*, p. 183.
[2] Op. cit. p. 185.

inconsistent combination, over the past forty years. For the very vigour of the public debates on strategy at different times during that period had arisen from the lack of thought on the part of the Government itself. The two potential enemies, throughout the second half of the nineteenth century, had been Russia and France. But war with the former was thought likely to turn, at least initially, on the defence of India; and in contemplating attack by the latter, Governments had wavered over the decades between reliance on the land and on the sea forces. The physical evidence bore witness to the succession of changing ideas: the forts around Portsmouth and on the Downs to the predominance of the land view with Palmerston and later with Stanhope; the new Fleet of the nineties, and the launching of the *Dreadnought*, to the revival of 'blue-water' doctrines. But the two rival conceptions had never been reconciled; improvements in one Service had been made without reference to the functions of the other; and the army, under such circumstances, was poised uneasily between two different but equal commitments, one in Asia and one at home.

The most recent definition of policy for the army, which at the beginning of the century was generally, though tacitly, assumed in Whitehall to represent the basis of national strategy, was the Stanhope Memorandum of 1891. That document, produced by the then Secretary of State for War, divided the principal duties of the army between home defence—of which it was taken as the guarantor—and the defence of India and certain Colonial strong points. When these commitments and 'their financial obligations' had been met, the army should aim at providing two corps for service overseas outside India. 'But it will be distinctly understood', the memorandum stated, 'that the possibility of the employment of an army corps in the field in any European war is sufficiently improbable to make it the primary duty of the military authorities to organize our forces efficiently for the defence of this country.'[1]

This policy held good until Haldane countermanded it in January 1906. The circumstances in which he did so illustrate the working of the system of defence at the time. Haldane did not act without support from prior events. In May 1905, Balfour had begun the process by stating in the House of Commons that the Government relied on the Fleet to protect the country from invasion.[2] This revision of policy, thus voiced publicly for the first time, reflected the satisfaction with the recent and current naval programmes, and the favour now enjoyed by the theories of the blue-water school. It was also made in the knowledge that the Admiralty now looked on Germany rather than on France as the potential enemy, and had recently begun to consider plans for that contingency. But matters had not rested there. Between the beginning of November 1905 and the end of January 1906, the conversations began between the War Office and the French Ministry of War which were to continue, with varying degrees of vigour, until 1914. Their basis, from the start, was the possibility of a British force operating in concert with the French on the Continent in the event of

[1] Maurice, *Haldane*, vol. 1, p. 171.

[2] The later modification of this policy, which returned to the army a greater share in the responsibility for countering invasion, does not invalidate the consequences of his statement at the time.

a war with Germany. Thus, within nine months the role of the army had become subject to a complete change. It was publicly recognized as no longer the first line of defence against invasion; and the possibility of its employment in the field in a European war had risen from bottom of the list to something very like the top.

The course of the early conversations with the French was not conveyed formally either to the Committee of Imperial Defence or to the Cabinet. The former, however, was concerned as early as August 1905 in the problems raised by a landing on the Continent, having indeed set on foot the first study by the War Office of such a possibility after considering a paper from the French; and in January 1906 it approved that Department's initial scheme. It seems likely, moreover, that a certain amount was known unofficially of what was going on, although the fear of opposition from some powerful members prevented the matter from being formally raised or discussed. But, to whatever extent the Committee of Imperial Defence was in fact aware of these developments, we must not exaggerate its responsibility for the decisions that followed. It did not—as it could not —instruct the Secretary of State for War to countermand the Stanhope Memorandum; nor did it endorse the subsequent reorganization of the forces until that reorganization had reached an advanced stage. Indeed, valuable as the Committee's support undoubtedly was to the Minister in these important years, a closer scrutiny suggests that his support was at least of equal value to it.

In the first place, the Committee's response in this instance was to a sudden and urgent threat, whose consequences it did not proceed to investigate systematically for some time. Its attention was still engaged for the most part by the traditional problem of the defence of India in the north, a last preoccupation with the Russian menace in Asia which in fact accounted for over half of its papers between 1904 and 1907.[1] It was not until November of the latter year that it turned to consider the effect of a European war on British and Imperial strategy, with an inquiry into the risks of invasion from Germany, which was followed by two inquiries into the nature of defence in the Middle East, and by a third—and for the first time extended—investigation, by a powerful sub-committee, of the problems attending a British intervention on the Continent. 'The phase of policy', as Lord Hankey has called it,[2] thus did not begin until almost two years after the War Office had begun to reorganize the army around an expeditionary force for Europe, and was not concluded until the autumn of 1909, when that process was irrevocably under way.

But the Committee's position in 1906 was shown more clearly by the reaction of the navy. The First Sea Lord, Admiral Fisher, was known to have had a detailed naval plan prepared for war with Germany, which was thought to run counter to the plans of the army. But contact between the two Departments on these matters was limited to conversations between the Director of

[1] The shift of public interest, as reflected in fiction, seems to have started slightly earlier. *Kim* and John Buchan's early book *The Half-Hearted*, both published in 1900, must be among the last novels catering for an informed public to take for their theme the Russian threat to the Northern Frontier. Erskine Childers' *The Riddle of the Sands*, in 1903, was the most popular example of the new school.

[2] The Rt Hon. Lord Hankey, *Government Control in War* (1945), p. 24.

Naval Intelligence and the Director of Military Operations; and when the Committee of Imperial Defence asked the First Sea Lord for his plans, he refused to divulge them or to guarantee the passage of an expeditionary force across the Channel. In the absence of action by the Prime Minister, neither the Committee nor the War Office could challenge this attitude; and although in 1907 Haldane induced Campbell-Bannerman to demand the production of the naval plans, neither body made any attempt thereafter to reconcile them with those of the army, or to seek from the Admiralty a closer degree of co-operation.

In the second half of the decade, indeed, the study of strategy at the centre, increasingly valuable as it became, depended for its value on the co-operation of the War Office. The very fact that such questions were referred to the Committee of Imperial Defence and not to the Cabinet, which remained largely ignorant of them, deprived the former of the latter's direct support, and increased its reliance, at this stage, on the goodwill of the Departments. This reliance was the more marked when the Prime Minister himself was not—as Campbell-Bannerman for much of his Premiership was not—particularly interested in the subject; and it accordingly seems no exaggeration to say that the progress of the Committee of Imperial Defence, at least from 1906 to 1908, was made possible by Haldane, who at the Prime Minister's request acted largely for him on the Committee, and drew it and the War Office into an increasingly intimate partnership. It was indeed fortunate, as the example of the Admiralty showed, that at this critical stage in the Committee's history, when the foundations were laid for its continued existence, the Secretary for War should have been in complete control of his Department, and should have been so strong a supporter of the central body.

Thus enabled to fulfil its functions of study and advice, the Committee developed fast. As was perhaps inevitable, membership, though in principle settled by invitation from the Prime Minister, tended to become standard. The Service Ministers and their professional advisers, the Foreign Secretary, the Chancellor of the Exchequer, the Secretaries of State for India and the Colonies, attended regularly. So too, after a time, did others with personal rather than official qualifications. Thus, in the last few years before the war Morley and Haldane continued to sit, after becoming Lord President and Lord Chancellor respectively, by virtue of their earlier service at the India Office and the War Office; and from 1906 to 1914, one of the Committee's most valuable members was Lord Esher, who held no Ministerial appointment. But this increase in membership, while ministering to the importance of the Committee, and indeed reflecting the anxiety of some members of the Cabinet to attend, was not always relevant to the nature of the business, and may have tended—at least according to Haldane—to subordinate the professional element to the political, contrary to the original intention. There was accordingly a marked development in these years of a system of sub-Committees, which indeed in the last few years before the war did most of the important work. By 1914, some thirty sub-Committees had been set up,

at different times and to study problems *ad hoc*; and
in addition there were five standing bodies—the Oversea Defence Committee, formerly the Colonial Defence
Committee; the Home Ports sub-Committee, the inheri-
tor of the Joint Naval and Military Committee of
Defence; the Air Committee; the Standing Technical
sub-Committee; and the Standing Committee on the
Co-ordination of Departmental Action on the Outbreak
of War, which produced the famous War Book for
August 1914.

The sub-Committees succeeded, as was their design,
in giving greater scope to the professional members than
those enjoyed on the main Committee; and, as Haldane
later claimed, this was perhaps the Liberal Government's
most useful contribution to the system. They also fostered
the importance of the secretariat, which co-ordinated
their work and, particularly through the Standing Committee on Departmental Action, linked the system itself
with a wide range of government. Their development,
indeed, reflected the nature of the Committee's business,
as 'the phase of policy' gave way to 'the phase of plans
and preparations':[1] a process which favoured the professional element, and brought the central system into
contact with the Departments at the official as well as at
the Ministerial level.

A somewhat similar development could be observed in
Imperial affairs, which were now contributing greatly to
raise the stature, and consolidate the position, of the
Committee of Imperial Defence. The process may be
observed particularly from 1907. At the Colonial Con-

[1] Hankey, *Government Control in War*, p. 26.

ference in that year, the self-governing Colonies were presented with a series of papers, based on the recent work at the War Office, which together amounted to a programme for Imperial co-ordination in strategy, organization and supply, between equal partners under advice from the British Government. The restriction of this programme to guidance and co-ordination, the fact that Britain did not ask for forces from the Dominions—as they were called from 1907—and that she did not claim control in any respect, commended the design to the different Governments; and they at once accepted it, and the recommendation, which it contained, for a General Staff to advise them all.

With the provision of this Staff, the pace began to quicken; and when, in 1909, a Naval and Military Conference was held in London on Imperial defence, the experts were able to make real headway: in naval affairs, on the responsibilities of a central Fleet to outlying communities within the Empire; in military affairs, on the standardization of forces and equipment, and on the development of what now became known as the Imperial General Staff. Visits by senior British officers further stimulated progress in the separate Dominions; and by the time that the Imperial Conference met in 1911, this varied professional activity had laid the foundations for a closer contact in defence between the Governments themselves. As was appropriate, this now became the concern explicitly of the Committee of Imperial Defence. For the first time, no items affecting defence were placed on the agenda of the Conference, but all were reserved, according to their nature, for the Committee or for the

Imperial General Staff. The Committee of Imperial Defence had in fact become, as Balfour had intended, the forum for the Imperial polity in this sphere; and as communication between the separate Dominions and London grew steadily closer in the years remaining before the war, it was on the Committee and the Staff, as complementary parts of a single structure, that it concentrated, at a pace and with results that had not been approached before.

Fortified by these experiences, at home and in the Empire, the central system had gained greatly in strength when, in the summer of 1911, the next serious scare of war arose. The measure of its development could indeed then be seen in its relations with, again, a recalcitrant Admiralty. For that Department, which seven years before had been taken as the model for a reformed War Office, had now been left behind by its pupil. While the influence of a General Staff could be observed increasingly in the army, there was still no central Staff for the navy; and although the faith in the Fleet as a fighting instrument remained as high as before, this lack of a thinking organ at the Admiralty was beginning to cause unease, to the staff of the Committee of Imperial Defence and to a few— though still only a few—eager spirits in the navy itself. When the late Admiral Sir Herbert Richmond, then a Commander, was courting his future wife in the middle years of the decade, 'the chief thing', she has recalled, 'I remember about our conversations was his outlining to me with fervour his plans for a Naval General Staff';[1]

[1] G. M. Trevelyan, 'Admiral Sir Herbert Richmond, 1871–1946', in *Proceedings of the British Academy*, vol. XXXII (1946), p. 328.

and in 1908 the new Secretary of the Committee of Imperial Defence, himself a sailor, admitted that, in the absence of such a Staff, 'not one naval officer out of fifty has any knowledge what a British Fleet will have to do in war, or how it will do it'.[1] In October 1909, as a result of the recent Beresford Enquiry in which the lack of such a body had been criticized, the Admiralty made an ostensible concession to the critics by forming a War Council. But this in fact proved to be a camouflage; the Council was purely advisory to the First Sea Lord, and its composition—the First Sea Lord presiding over the Assistant Secretary of the Admiralty, the Director of Naval Intelligence and a new Director of Mobilization—showed clearly enough that the new body was not designed to be very formidable.

The lack of a Naval Staff had now indeed come to reflect, and to support, the paramountcy of the First Sea Lord himself. In 1904, his powers had been increased in relation to those of the other Sea Lords; and for the next few years at least, strategic direction in practice lay entirely in his hands. Nor, while Fisher held the appointment, was he prepared to see the position changed. The results were seen again in the course of 1909, when another, though less serious, scare of war with Germany arose. At the beginning of the year, Fisher was once more determined, as in 1906, not to confide the naval plans to the Committee of Imperial Defence; and although, as a result of the Beresford Enquiry, he was later obliged to do so in outline, when the Committee pressed

---

[1] Maurice, *Haldane*, vol. 1, p. 243. The Secretary was then Captain (later Rear-Admiral) Sir Charles Ottley.

him for details in November he staged an outburst which effectually quelled any further invasion of the Admiralty's privacy. But this proved to be the last occasion on which such an attitude was possible. By the end of 1909, the Committee had received from the War Office the first detailed scheme for the deployment of an expeditionary force in north-west Europe; and when in 1911 the Agadir crisis produced a fresh threat of immediate war, that commitment had become probable enough to make a detailed co-ordination of plans between the Services urgent and inevitable.

The issue was settled following the famous meeting of the Committee itself, summoned by the Prime Minister for 23 August. The story has been recounted more than once, most fully by Sir Winston Churchill. As the meeting proceeded, it became increasingly clear that the Services' plans differed radically from each other, and could not be reconciled; and although the debate was inconclusive, the result was soon to show clearly that the War Office view had prevailed. In the event, plans were allowed to go ahead for the passage of an expeditionary force to France, with which the Admiralty was obliged to conform.

The meeting of 23 August is of interest, for the effect on the Admiralty and for the light it throws on the position which the Committee now occupied as an element of government. The consequences for the navy were soon apparent. For soon after the meeting, Haldane informed the Prime Minister that, as Secretary for War in the conditions that now prevailed, he must demand 'a sweeping reform' at the Admiralty; and as a result Mr Churchill

47

was sent to the Department, charged, in co-operation with Haldane himself, with the task of forming a Naval Staff. The consequences, when war came, were not particularly satisfactory: partly because the new instrument had not had time to settle down; partly because Churchill failed to carry the sailors with him as Haldane had carried the soldiers; and partly because the new Chief of the Staff did not become the principal professional adviser to his Minister, as the Chief of the General Staff had been designated at the War Office in 1904, but remained separate from the First Sea Lord, with a consequent ambiguity in the relations between the three authorities. Nevertheless, the somewhat disappointing result does not detract from the achievement of the Committee of Imperial Defence, in bringing the most independent of Departments at last within the orbit of a national plan for war, and in fostering, as a direct consequence, the formation of a Naval Staff to parallel the General Staff for the army.

The fact that it was the Committee, and not the Cabinet, which had been summoned on 23 August also raised, more directly than before, the question of its relations with that body. For some time, some members of the Cabinet had been uneasy about the Committee, and the Agadir crisis did nothing to lessen their suspicions. 'It had not made a war yet, but the experience of 1911 showed that it easily might.'[1] How far important members of the Cabinet, who from time to time sat on the Committee, were cognizant of all its business, is difficult to say. Lord Morley, for instance, one of the most regular

[1] Sir Almeric Fitzroy, *Memoirs*, vol. II (n.d., but 1925), p. 539.

of attendants for many years, later claimed that he had not been aware of the course of the conversations with the French, although both Asquith and Haldane have pointed out that he was present on some at least of the most important relevant occasions. But that such a conflict of evidence should exist points, perhaps, the true nature of the case. For the questions referred to the Committee were not only such as to demand treatment by a body other than the Cabinet as then constituted, but were not of the type that normally interested a Cabinet in the conditions prevailing before the First World War. It was thus possible even for Ministers concerned in the affairs of both bodies to relegate the problems of the Committee to the place they occupied in the Cabinet's attention; while to the generality of Ministers, involved in the claims and implications of a period interested primarily in social reform, such problems scarcely existed apart from their effect on the national budget. In these circumstances, the Committee grew as an alternative rather than as a complement to the Cabinet in matters of defence; and as such matters became intermittently more prominent in the closing years of peace, both their growing prominence and their intermittence led some Ministers to regard the Committee with suspicion, as a somewhat irregular vehicle for the operations of some of their colleagues.

It had certainly proved a vehicle for those of the Prime Minister. For his predominance on the Committee was as marked in 1914 as it had been at the start. At different times in its brief history, fears had been expressed that the nature of the business must give undue power to the professional members. But in fact, as Sydenham Clarke noted later, any such increase in power must derive from, and depend on, the motion of the Prime Minister himself; and in the event, particularly under Balfour before 1906 and Asquith after 1908, it was he whose authority was strengthened within the machinery of government. That does not mean to say that it was strengthened correspondingly within the Cabinet. The relations of a Prime Minister with his colleagues are normally formed more immediately by character and political circumstance than by administrative developments. But it meant that the Prime Minister had a powerful instrument to hand should the political circumstances, and his own character, encourage him to use it.

By the outbreak of the First World War, the Committee of Imperial Defence had thus acquired some marked characteristics, whose combination should be examined before we proceed to the war itself. For that combination may help us to understand the developments in organization which followed so quickly, so adversely and, as it may seem, in some ways so inexplicably. Where the pre-war Committee has been criticized in the light of later events, it has usually been for its neglect of economic and industrial preparation. But such a criticism is not entirely to the point. The Committee had in fact broken fresh ground, in preparing legislation on trade with the enemy and arrangements for insuring shipping; the industrial preparations required immediately by the type of operations envisaged were primarily the concern of the Service Departments, and not of the Committee; and it was scarcely to be expected, given the prevalent conception and capacities of government, that their subsequent effects on industry and finance would have been foreseen at all precisely, or that a central organ would have been allowed to do much even in the way of general preparation. That would have demanded an adaptation and extension of the existing system of intelligence and control, for unfamiliar purposes, which would have been considered certainly illegitimate and probably impossible. On the other hand, the early failure of the system of defence for its accustomed purpose of strategic control demands some explanation. For how was it that despite the development of an organization, hailed at the time and later as inaugurating new methods in the strategic sphere, authority should have been exercised so inadequately once war began, and with results, moreover, that in some respects showed a reversion to earlier practices which the pre-war system had been concerned to overcome?

The answer must lie, in great part, in the development of the system itself. As we have seen, the Committee of Imperial Defence was stronger for some purposes than for others; and those purposes were not necessarily the most important when war had been declared. While it is therefore true to say, as Lord Hankey has said, that 'our . . . system of Government control throughout two major wars has been evolved from this Committee',[1] that evolution would not necessarily be foreseen in 1914. For three things must be remembered about the Committee's early history. First, it had been established and elaborated as a system of study and review, not as a system of

[1] Hankey, loc. cit. p. 22.

authority. And while it had in fact, in pursuing those objects, placed authority where it must lie, and had evolved principles which would satisfy the demands of responsible control when called upon to do so, this could not easily be envisaged from the experience of the Committee hitherto. That experience had accustomed Ministers to the idea of a smaller, more expert body for the review of strategic affairs; but the precise role of such a body, in relation to others with greater constitutional authority, had not been, and probably could not be, foreseen when the study of strategy gave way suddenly to the conduct of war.

But secondly, this reviewing function of the Committee had itself tended, in the later years, to be overshadowed by purely administrative functions. For while the Committee had been set up to consider problems of strategy in general, it had become increasingly involved in the detailed preparations for a specific campaign, and its organization had been adjusted increasingly to that end. In the process, it had achieved notable results. It had fostered study and co-ordination in military affairs between the different parts of the Empire, in a way that no other body could probably have equalled. It had elaborated new methods of business, far superior to those of the Cabinet itself and later to form an essential aspect of the processes of central control. It had brought a small but influential and growing group of serving officers into closer contact with the higher levels of administration, a development which in time was to bring the Service Staffs, as the last sector of government, within the orbit of administrative standards already prevailing elsewhere.

It had in turn brought the Civil Service more closely into touch with problems of defence as an aspect of central government. And, perhaps most important, it had laid such problems more directly before an inner group of Ministers, and had thereby helped to change the climate of political interest, which largely sets the climate for administration. But, far-reaching as these achievements were, they did not seem applicable to the most immediate problems of control facing a system of authority under the pressure of war.

And thirdly, it must be remembered that, under such pressure, neither the Cabinet nor the Services would necessarily be influenced very much by the example or implications of a committee which had affected them so far only in certain respects, and then intermittently. For although the Committee of Imperial Defence had done much valuable work, and was regarded as important, its influence with the Departments was by no means complete or automatic, while as an aspect of Cabinet government it was uncertain and somewhat suspect. Opinion was not settled on its usefulness, or even on its desirability; and it was certainly far from occupying a place at all comparable with that which it occupied later in any consideration of the practice of government. It was rather a somewhat irregular body, which had developed along certain definite lines for certain increasingly specific purposes, and which, so far from providing an obvious system of authority for the Cabinet in war, was limited in its influence both with the Cabinet and with the Services, and indeed enjoyed a status that was not entirely secure.

The consequences were displayed in the course of the first two years of the war. For the history of the Liberal and First Coalition Governments until the end of 1916 is the history of a search for a viable form of authority in unfamiliar circumstances. As Asquith later remarked, 'the root difficulty in the early conduct of the War...was how to combine rapid and effective executive action in the various theatres with the maintenance of Cabinet responsibility and control'.[1] This problem was bound to assume a novel form in the first great European war for this country in a hundred years. It proved to be one for which, as it seemed, pre-war experience could not provide an adequate solution. The difficulties were indeed revealed at the very outset, at a meeting summoned by the Cabinet on 5 August 1914 to advise it on the immediate military measures. As had become the case in the Committee of Imperial Defence, this was attended by some outside figures, summoned for the occasion. But while such attendance was useful and desirable in a deliberative and consultative body, it was the reverse when decisions had to be taken by a responsible authority. The meeting, in fact, marked the start of that formless search for professional advice, based on no proper system, which was henceforward to distinguish the conduct of the central bodies. The pre-war example was obscuring the position, by the application of methods developed for one purpose to another essentially different from it.

The process continued as it had begun. On the same day that the Cabinet summoned its advisory meeting, the

[1] The Earl of Oxford and Asquith, *Memories and Reflections, 1852–1927*, vol. II (1928), p. 23.

first, and least well known, of its new War Committees was set up—the 'Joint Naval and Military Committee for the Consideration of Combined Operations in Foreign Territories', or the 'Offensive sub-Committee of the Committee of Imperial Defence' as it was more often called. Its deliberations were confined to ventures against German colonial possessions, while the Secretary for War and the Commander-in-Chief, India began their own correspondence on operations in Asia, and the Committee of Imperial Defence continued to supervise the concentration of the British Expeditionary Force in France. These separate strategic compartments, each the concern of a different authority, reflected the emphasis of the pre-war system on a single dominant object, and its unsuitability, owing to the varying membership and size of the Committee, for co-ordinating operations as a whole. When the first battles had been fought in France, the Committee of Imperial Defence itself therefore faded away, to be summoned only on occasions to study questions of home defence. The Offensive sub-Committee also disappeared, and a new War Council was set up, to review the strategic situation as a whole. Its membership resembled in principle the normal regular attendance at the pre-war Committee of Imperial Defence—the Prime Minister in the chair, with the Service Ministers, the Foreign Secretary, the Chancellor of the Exchequer and Lord Balfour, attended regularly by the First Sea Lord and the C.I.G.S. The Secretary of State for India and the Lord Chancellor, Haldane, were soon added, together with Admiral of the Fleet Sir Arthur Wilson as a naval elder statesman. This body in turn gave way, in June 1915, to the Dardanelles Committee, set up initially to deal with that venture and gradually drawn into dealing with the British strategy as a whole. Its composition reflected that of the new Coalition Government, with five Ministers from the former Administration and five Conservatives, attended regularly by the professional heads of the Services. In November 1915, when the Dardanelles campaign had obviously failed, this Committee was replaced by a fresh War Committee, which settled at first at six members but later rose to eleven, again attended regularly by the First Sea Lord and the C.I.G.S.

The similarities between these three bodies were greater than the differences. The Dardanelles and War Committees met more regularly than the earlier War Council, which was called only to review departures in policy or questions specifically submitted to it; and the handling of business, as we shall see, improved greatly in the War Committee compared with its two predecessors. But the Committees shared a number of fundamental characteristics, some of which derived from the Committee of Imperial Defence. Each approximated, in the end, to the size and composition of the pre-war body; each continued to summon outside opinion when required, so that attendance was flexible and varied; and each relied on a secretariat to organize its business and keep it in touch with other bodies. Nor were these similarities surprising; for the early wartime Committees were in fact designed explicitly to reproduce the functions of the Committee of Imperial Defence, 'with', in Hankey's words, 'more executive authority'. But here lay the difficulty. For while the Committees might adopt the methods of their predecessor, those methods were not in themselves capable of meeting the new demands of control in war. Admirably suited as they might be to serve an effective system of authority, they were not a substitute for that system, as Ministers at the time seemed inclined to think. The dilemma was pointed by Asquith in the House of Commons in 1915. 'I think', he then said, 'a Committee such as I have indicated ought to be clothed with power to take...decisions, and to act upon them. On the other hand, I am very jealous of the maintenance of collective Cabinet responsibility for large changes and new departures in policy; but I believe that in practice it will be found perfectly capable of working out two things together.'[1] Unfortunately, it was not. Indeed, the reverse was the case. For not only did the retention of supreme authority by the larger Cabinet deprive the Committees of the power for which their organization would have suited them admirably: it also reduced their value as organs of study and advice. The fact that the pre-war Committee of Imperial Defence had developed as an alternative to, rather than as a regular instrument of, the Cabinet in strategic affairs, now left a constitutional gap. And that gap became the more marked as political conditions deteriorated, and as the needs of a Coalition Government sought satisfaction within an already ineffective Committee. The expert forum then became less expert, while the Cabinet, composed of the same divergent elements as those that composed the Committee, was the more determined to retain its active control. By the end of 1915, the Committee had

[1] *Parliamentary Debates (Fifth Series)*, vol. LXXV, col. 526.

thus lost much of the original deliberative power, without gaining in any way in executive authority.

As had been demonstrated before, and as was to be demonstrated again, weakness at one level caused weakness at others; and the Committees' lack of power in relation to the Cabinet was paralleled, and increased, by their lack of power in relation to the Service Departments. The position was illustrated, as it was largely shaped, by the history of Kitchener at the War Office. The appointment of an eminent soldier as Secretary of State on the outbreak of war marked a departure from orthodox methods. It at once contributed to their failure, with Kitchener's virtual domination of an uncertain Cabinet and with his virtual abolition of the General Staff. For the pre-war Staff had been sent—and it is a reflection of the way in which it was regarded—almost in its entirety to France; and its absence allowed the new Secretary of State, unfamiliar with recent practice, to impose his highly personal methods upon the Department. The C.I.G.S. became a subordinate to a superior officer; his status as First Military Member of the Army Council, laid down in 1904,[1] was quietly abandoned; and, in the persons of Douglas and Wolfe Murray, he and his organization lost all initiative in the formulation of strategy. Kitchener thus reigned supreme at the War Office; while at the Admiralty, the ambiguity already existing between the powers of the Minister and those of the First Sea Lord over the Staff[2] was increased by the dispute between Churchill and Fisher in 1915. In the spring and summer of that year, the position was

[1] See p. 32 above.   [2] See p. 48 above.

accordingly as Balfour later described it: '. . . the principal actors at home were a soldier without strategical genius, who controlled the military machine, a sailor equally without strategical genius, who ought to have controlled, but did not, the naval machine, and a brilliant amateur who attempted, but failed, to dominate both.'[1] The amalgamation of Ministerial and professional functions at the War Office, and the struggle between them at the Admiralty, were equally unfortunate; and as a result every aspect of Staff work was in disarray. The War Office had reverted towards its position of over ten years before; the Naval Staff was increasingly bedevilled by disagreement from above; there could be no joint Staff work between the Departments; and thus no provision of an informed Staff thought to serve a central committee of the Cabinet. It was, for instance, typical of the times that Kitchener, Churchill and the Dardanelles Committee should all have neglected, when discussing the initial plans for forcing the Straits, the reports existing in the pre-war files of the War Office and the Committee of Imperial Defence which showed the effects of bombarding shore batteries with 16-inch naval guns and smaller howitzers.

This confusion in London could not but affect relations between the central authorities and those in the theatres. The most notorious result was to be seen in the Dardanelles campaign, which provided a classic example of what can happen to a conjunct operation when no clear plan is available beforehand, and when the lack of an adequate system leaves strong personalities free to settle

[1] Dugdale, *Balfour*, vol. II, p. 184.

59

the division of responsibilities between the Government and the men on the spot. But other theatres had similar, if less dramatic, experiences. The early failure of the campaign in Mesopotamia was due largely to the fact that it was conducted by an India Command responsible to a curious trinity of the Viceroy's Council, the India Office and the Secretary of State for War in his personal capacity, with neither the Army Council nor the General Staff at the War Office concerned, and with the Cabinet, as usual, intervening at different times in differing degrees. And on the Western Front, the Chief of Staff, Sir William Robertson, was driven by the irregular nature of his communications with London to suggest in June 1915 that the C.I.G.S. should resume his pre-war functions, and that the War Council itself should be overhauled. That such proposals, affecting the Cabinet as well as the Department, should come from such a quarter, pointed the situation. Commanders were not only being weakened in their own sphere by the Government's activities: they were being brought, with undue prominence, into the Government's affairs.

Thus awkwardly constructed, the system of strategic direction could only respond in a series of jerks to fast-moving events. It was significant that the Cabinet Committees, which resembled each other so closely, should so often have changed their names. When the emphasis lay on the concentration of the Expeditionary Force in France and on raids against the German colonies, the Committee of Imperial Defence and its Offensive sub-Committee sufficed. When that phase had passed, a War Council appeared. When the Dardanelles campaign came to the fore, the War Council was succeeded by a Dardanelles Committee. And when the Dardanelles declined in priority, that Committee gave way to a War Committee. This was not flexibility, but rather the reaction of an inadequate system to situations as they arose.

In the course of 1916, the situation changed again, this time radically and decisively; and the central organization began to move, with increasing speed, in a fresh response. Not its least momentous line of development then lay beyond the military sphere. In the earlier part of the war, the Government's economic activities are of greater interest to the economic than to the constitutional historian. New economic needs were coming into existence, some of which raised new administrative problems. But they demanded institutional satisfaction over a wide field only when the war had continued for some time. In the first year to eighteen months, we can therefore distinguish clearly, for our purposes, between sectors of the economy which later became subject increasingly to the same kind of management, and can trace different effects on different parts of the Departmental system.

Governments in war make two demands on the national economy: to produce enough men, munitions and equipment to meet the objects of their strategy; and to do so without endangering, materially or financially, the structure on which those supplies depend. But to state the matter in these terms is to point the revolution which has occurred in the application of economic thought since 1914. In the earlier part of the First World War, the measures of the British Government were taken in the belief that the demands of the forces could be met, given the appropriate action, out of the capacity of the economy as it stood. Nor was such an assumption so absurd as it may have seemed a few years later. Most of the military and civil authorities looked forward at the outset, for different reasons, to a very short war, and the army had been formed and equipped deliberately on that basis. Nor, when such a hope had been disappointed, was the subsequent long and static struggle by any means certain until the Dardanelles campaign had failed. It is indeed interesting to speculate on the possible effects for administrative and economic thought had that campaign succeeded and its anticipated results followed. In 1914 and 1915 the British economy was in fact buoyant; and given a war of under two years' duration, it was not beyond its capacity to supply what was wanted without a major disturbance. For the Government to have tried, in that period, to mobilize its resources comprehensively would therefore have been unnecessary and, being unnecessary, unpopular.

'Business as usual', with its financial concomitant, was thus a reasonable and indeed inevitable policy at the outbreak of war; and perhaps remained not unreasonable for longer than has sometimes been supposed. We must in fact distinguish at this stage, as the Government distinguished in practice, between the problems of production and those of distribution. The former soon demanded an answer: the latter, by and large, did not. Indeed the difficulties of distribution were caused, for almost two years, not by a shortage of material but by disturbances to prices and to the pattern of employment.

It was, for instance, the rising price of freights over that period which was mainly responsible for the Government's growing supervision of the shipping industry. It was the sudden rise in the price of food, followed by its stabilization, which first led, and then confined, the Government to the establishment of a cost-of-living index. And it was the need to strike a balance between the demands of the forces and those of munitions which in the second half of 1915 produced the attempts to record, but not as yet to supervise, the distribution of labour as a whole.

Such disturbances lay within the compass, albeit extended, of existing administrative methods; and the traditional organs were able to expand and adapt themselves to the demands. The Board of Trade remained the Department principally concerned in the supply and treatment of material and labour outside the munitions' industry, associated with the Admiralty for shipping, with the War Office for certain materials and articles of food, and with the Home Office and the Local Government Board for questions affecting employment. Treasury control followed familiar lines, and the various Commissions and special bodies created to deal with special cases—such as the Royal Commission on Sugar Supplies, the Fair Wages and Reserved Occupations Committees, the Requisitioning (Carriage of Foodstuffs) and Ship Licensing Committees—were included or entirely involved in the existing Departmental machinery. Within the old Departments new branches were taking root, from some of which new institutions would later emerge. But it was not until the end of 1916 that those institutions began to appear, to alter significantly the Departmental system itself.

In the field of production, however, that development had by then taken place. With the adoption in August 1914 of Kitchener's immediate programme of thirty divisions, it was clear that the armaments' industry must expand at once. The War Office indeed then proposed that it should be nationalized. But this, even if it had been politically feasible, would have raised administrative difficulties which the War Office itself could probably not have solved, and the first demands were in fact dealt with along the familiar lines. The lesser expansion of naval munitions was similarly handled within the confines of the Admiralty. The two Departments operated virtually without supervision. A Cabinet Committee on Munitions was set up in August, which proved useful to the War Office in the first few months in settling targets, in confirming the decision to rely on the existing armaments' firms, and in supporting the demands upon them. But thereafter the Committee seldom intervened, and the pre-war organization was allowed to stand in its essentials until the eve of the great shell scandal in May 1915.

In March of that year, however, an attempt was made to secure more adequate control over the two Departments. The Cabinet then set up a new Munitions of War Committee, under the chairmanship of Lloyd George, designed to co-ordinate policy for the two services, and —a significant step—to supervise the programme for the army through the medium of a new Armaments Output Committee, situated within the War Office and under the chairmanship of the Secretary of State, but designated by the Cabinet Committee as its executive agent. The shift in responsibility was moreover soon underlined, for in April the chairman of the Cabinet Committee authorized the two executive heads of the War Office Committee to act from day to day 'without reference to the Secretary of State'. It was not surprising that these anomalies were soon judged to be unacceptable, and that an entirely new organ was created. In June 1915 the first Munitions of War Act was passed, setting up a Ministry of Munitions independent of the War Office.[1]

At first the new Ministry was far from being master in its own house. But in the course of a few months its powers developed fast, particularly in relation to those of the War Office. In August, it gained control of the Royal Ordnance Factories; in September, it was made responsible for all expenditure on munitions; and in November, it secured the transfer of the Ordnance Board, responsible for design. The prominence of munitions as a political issue, the fact that Lloyd George, appointed Minister, was well alive to the problems involved, and the growth within the Ministry—which he did much to promote— of a more effective partnership between civil servants and industrialists, soon ensured that the Department would fill the place for which it had been designed. More elaborate, and sometimes fresh techniques, closer links with the industry and its regional organizations, and above all the need to legislate for the great labour questions involved, brought together in a new way

---

[1] The Ministry of Munitions broke new ground in another way. It was the first Department to be given the title of 'Ministry'.

problems hitherto considered separately. It was not only that the Ministry of Munitions was doing old things better. It was finding itself obliged to do new things, and to develop new skills in the process.

This was particularly true of the Ministry's supervision of its manpower. In July 1915 it took over from the Service Departments the protection of the necessary labour. At the same time, it inherited from them and the Treasury the responsibility for negotiating terms of employment. The Labour Regulations, in the Act which created the Ministry, extended the Treasury Agreement of April 1915, and formed the first comprehensive code for labour in a large sector of industry. The implications for manpower as a whole were not yet obvious. It was not until the failure of voluntary recruitment for the forces at the end of the year that general priorities had to be studied, and action taken upon them. But when that need arose, the Ministry's experience proved of great value to the other interests concerned—so much so, indeed, that it found itself surrendering some responsibilities to new organs inheriting many of its features. In this and other ways, the Ministry of Munitions was in fact a portent, and one which was soon to be followed as the effects of the war began to spread beyond production to the life of the country.

CHAPTER III

THE SYSTEM EXTENDED AND REMODELLED, 1916–18

In December 1916, Asquith's First Coalition Government gave way to the Second Coalition under Lloyd George. Great changes in administration followed at once. Within a month, four new Ministries—Labour, Food, Shipping, and Pensions—and three new Departments— National Service, Scientific and Industrial Research, and Food Production—had been created, and the uneasy combination of Cabinet and War Committee had been replaced by a small War Cabinet. These measures heralded others, at home and in the Alliance; and the advent of Lloyd George to power has always, and rightly, been regarded as opening a new chapter in the history of British organization for war.

Innovations of this magnitude could not have been introduced so quickly had not both the conditions and the state of the existing system been considered ripe. Lloyd George's changes drew on experience accumulated in Asquith's time, and responded to a situation which itself had changed fundamentally. For if the turning point for administration came at the end of 1916, the turning point in the war had come a year before. It was then that the conflict entered on a new phase, and one whose implications were soon to be felt in almost every sphere. The failure to turn the enemy's flank by the end of 1915 rendered almost inevitable a war of attrition, in which, unless a war-winning weapon could be produced, victory would depend on the most effective application of a weight of resources. In the course of 1916, the symptoms of such a struggle were increasingly to be seen in Britain. Voluntary recruitment to the forces gave way to the first hesitant stages of compulsion. Shipping passages and space were controlled more closely. The first article of food was rationed. The small investor was involved for the first time directly in war finance, with the introduction of War Savings Certificates. The first British loan was floated in the United States. And on the Western Front itself, the battle of the Somme showed the sort of demands in men and material which static warfare might raise in future.

The balance of the Alliance, too, was changing under these demands. Hitherto, Britain's influence had been upheld by her naval supremacy and by the industrial and financial strength which it was recognized she could apply. But this latent strength was now becoming actual; while the 'coming of age' of the British army on the Somme witnessed a new balance in military strength itself. As the New Armies came to fruition, and began to take over an increasing proportion of the Allied line, the British power by land could no longer be considered subordinate to the French. When the consequences of war in the twentieth century were first displayed in 1916, it therefore seemed likely that Britain, of the Western Powers, would be best fitted to endure them.

The system of government which had fostered this growing strength was now proving inadequate to meet the tasks it raised. Two administrative processes may be observed over the last two years of the war: an extension and redistribution of Departmental powers, to cover and correspond more closely to new economic needs; and the remodelling of the central structure, to correlate the Departmental activities, to link them more effectively with the direction of strategy, and to present the results, in coherent form, as the British contribution to the Alliance. These two processes—in the Departments and at the centre—were naturally not pursued distinctly, or in strict chronological order. It was indeed Lloyd George's achievement to have brought them into a more satisfactory relationship from an incipient muddle. For in 1916, relations between the Cabinet and the Departments seemed to be growing confused and indeed somewhat obscure. The First Coalition Government was not slow to devise machinery for specific problems as they arose, nor was it unaware of the needs of the future. The Departments continued to develop new branches, and to improve their techniques; a new Ministry of Blockade, formed in January 1916, strengthened the system at a weak point; and the Cabinet itself set up a number of committees in cases where co-ordination seemed necessary. Nor were less obvious needs neglected. It is often forgotten, for instance, that it was Asquith who approved the formation of a Council of Scientific and Industrial Research, and the proposal for a committee to investigate the machinery of government. But while the Cabinet was anxious to improve the system, it did not possess the key. Its interventions more often than not succeeded only in adding to the difficulties which had caused them. The Shipping Committee, the Committee on Exemptions and its successor the Manpower Distribution Board, the Food Control Committee, all showed in different ways in 1916 the consequences of imposing on the Departments a series of *ad hoc* bodies with powers at once vague and limited. Instead of providing co-ordination and relief, the committees tended to duplicate and confuse. Cabinet control seemed to be failing at the point where it was needed, and by the very means it was accustomed to adopt.

The cause of this failure emerged only gradually. It was not indeed until the last year of the war that the reorganization in one sector of government, which by then had taken place, showed more clearly the pattern to be adopted in the other. For in fact it was useless to expect co-ordinating bodies to prove effective until the bodies to be co-ordinated had themselves been rendered so. The Departments must be remodelled before the inter-Departmental committees could function properly. Otherwise, as had been shown in the military sphere during the period of reform, the organs of control would merely reflect the confusion in the executive agencies, and there would be no proper link between policy and administration.

The exact nature of this link emerged slowly from experience. But at the end of 1916, Lloyd George saw clearly enough the need to strengthen the chain at either end. The New Ministries and Secretaries Act and its successors, by which the new agencies were created, affected the whole war sector of the earlier system. The new Ministry of Shipping involved changes in the Admiralty and the Board of Trade; the Ministry of

Labour in the Board of Trade, the Home Office, the Ministry of Munitions and the Local Government Board; the Ministry of Food and the Food Production Department in the Board of Agriculture; the Department of National Service in the Ministry of Munitions and the Service Departments. At the same time, the revised system provided a more effective means of extending Departmental authority to those new questions of national distribution which hitherto had lain outside the purview of government; and in so doing, strengthened the links between Whitehall and the non-statutory bodies which were becoming increasingly important in local and advisory capacities. Of course there were many obstacles to overcome, and some failures to record. But the redistribution of functions was in harmony with the needs, and improvements followed. In the course of 1917, the process was carried farther. The Department of National Service was remodelled as a Ministry, and in the summer a Ministry of Reconstruction was set up.

The Departmental changes were designed, as Lloyd George himself made clear, to strengthen the system of central control. The new body which he created in December 1916 marked, as is well known, a break with the past. Instead of a Cabinet of 23 members, in which all the great Departments were represented, there was a War Cabinet initially of five, later varying between five and seven,[1] of whom only one member—Bonar Law, as Chancellor of the Exchequer—held a Departmental

[1] The War Cabinet consisted of the following members on its formation in December 1916: Mr Lloyd George, Prime Minister and First Lord of the Treasury; Lord Curzon, Lord President of the Council; Mr Bonar

post. The others were freed from such responsibilities, so that they could, in Lord Hankey's words, 'give their whole time and energy to the central problems of the war'.[1] This prime duty was also thought to excuse the Prime Minister from handling the detail of Parliamentary business, and the leadership of the House of Commons was entrusted to Bonar Law as the leading member of the largest party in the Coalition. The War Cabinet was thus designed, as one authority has put it, as a Committee of Public Safety,[2] relying on the revised Departmental system to relieve it of the detail of administration, and on the existence of a Coalition to relieve it of the burden of Parliamentary duties.

The design could not be followed strictly in the event. If the shape of the Coalition allowed Lloyd George to depute the bulk of Parliamentary business to Bonar Law, it also obliged him to take care that his own interests did not suffer thereby; and indeed it is difficult to see how the devolution of political duties could have been carried so far in such circumstances with any other Conservative Minister. Nor was the daily press of administration excluded so completely as had been hoped. In 1917, 248 visitors attended meetings of the War Cabinet for items in which they were concerned; and, as both Smuts

Law, Chancellor of the Exchequer; Lord Milner and Mr Arthur Henderson, Ministers without Portfolio. Total membership, 5.

Thereafter, the following changes were made: General Smuts joined the War Cabinet in June 1917, 6. Sir Edward Carson joined in July, 1917, 7. Mr George Barnes replaced Mr Henderson in August 1917, 7. Sir Edward Carson and Mr Barnes left the War Cabinet in January 1918, 5. Lord Milner left the War Cabinet, and Mr Austen Chamberlain joined, in April 1918, 5.   [1] Hankey, loc. cit. p. 40.

[2] K. B. Smellie, *A Hundred Years of English Government* (2nd edn, 1950), p. 178.

and Hankey remarked in the late summer, it was becoming seriously overburdened with detail. This method of doing business reflected, indeed, a failure to foresee one consequence of the new system. For if the War Cabinet, designed to frame policy and co-ordinate administration, was to consist almost entirely of non-Departmental Ministers, how in practice were they to carry out those functions over bodies of which they were not the responsible heads? What in fact was to be the form of the connexion between the Cabinet and the Departments? It is interesting to see the terms in which the first Report of the War Cabinet dealt, or failed to deal, with this question. It seems to have assumed that the answer lay largely in the War Cabinet's new secretariat, which Lloyd George had transferred from the War Committee and which, in the words of the Report, 'provides...another means of securing touch between the War Cabinet and the various Government Departments'.[1] The provision of a staff for the Cabinet was certainly an event of great importance. It gave that body, and all its subordinate parts, proper means for the first time of preparing and handling their business, of recording the results, and of communicating them to those concerned. But, essential as these tasks were to the work of the supreme organ, the secretariat could not in itself act as a link in the chain of responsibility. Indeed, its authority and prestige derived very largely from the fact that it persistently disclaimed such a role. From early in its history, it was at pains to make clear that, like its predecessors with the Committee of Imperial Defence

[1] Cmd. 9005 (1918), p. 3.

and the War Committees, it was restricted to purely secretarial duties, and that it did not seek to encroach on the functions of the Departments and was not to be identified in any way with responsibility for the policy it was designed to record. The secretariat was a staff, not an authority. It oiled the wheels, it did not move the engine. Indispensable as it became to the processes of Cabinet government, it remained throughout a servant and not an element of government itself.

The link had therefore to be found elsewhere; and, as became increasingly apparent, it lay in a remodelled Committee system. The redistribution of Departmental powers, and the provision of a central staff, offered a better opportunity for inter-Departmental co-ordination; and in the course of 1917 this developed to some extent in the civil sphere. It was not, however, an obvious process at the start. If we take once more the evidence of the War Cabinet's Report for 1917, the position may be seen. The committees occupy little attention compared with the Departments; there is generally a failure to distinguish between those responsible to a Departmental Minister and those responsible to the Cabinet; and in the case of the latter, between *ad hoc* and standing bodies. The change twelve months later may be seen in the opening passage of the War Cabinet's next Report, for 1918.[1]

In the Report for 1917, it was described how a number of the less important but often highly complex questions were referred to individual members of the War Cabinet or to Committees of Ministers or others, sometimes with power to

[1] Cmd. 325 (1919), p. 1.

decide or sometimes for the purpose of carrying out detailed investigations on behalf of the War Cabinet, leaving the final decision for the Cabinet itself. The principal development in 1918 was in the extension of the system of permanent Committees to deal with groups of questions which previously had tended more and more to come within the range of subjects dealt with by particular members of the War Cabinet.

Here in fact was the necessary instrument of the small Cabinet in war, whose development over the next thirty years was to prove the most significant feature of Cabinet government. The moment of its recognition can be dated exactly. In December 1916, and again in May 1917, Cabinet committees had been formed   in the first instance the Committee on the Restriction of Imports, in the second the Tonnage Priority Committee—which in effect amounted to standing bodies. But they were not accepted for what they were, and the Cabinet itself dated the process to September 1917, when a new Aerial Operations Committee first met. This body had been formed to report to the War Cabinet on priorities in the manufacture of aircraft. But members soon found that the problems could not be studied in isolation, and they accordingly recommended that the Committee should be reconstituted, as a standing body, to study, settle and where necessary report on all priorities of manufacture. The War Cabinet agreed; and in October 1917 the War Priorities Committee was formed, the first standing committee of Cabinet in the civil sphere to be designated as such.

But the War Cabinet had been formed not only to coordinate the national effort more effectively, but to achieve a more vigorous conduct of the military effort itself. Throughout 1916, there had been a growing dissatisfaction with the Cabinet and the War Committee, and Lloyd George in particular had voiced, if spasmodically, the need for a change. The first proposal, which he himself seemed to favour and which held the field until a late stage, was that Asquith should remain Prime Minister, that the Cabinet should continue, under his chairmanship, to be the body constitutionally responsible to Parliament, but that executive responsibility for the day to day conduct of the war should be vested in a revised, small War Committee under the chairmanship of Lloyd George. The exact relations proposed between the chairman of the Committee and the Prime Minister underwent several changes in the course of the negotiations, and in any case it is hard to say how far Lloyd George himself really wanted such an arrangement. But its merits are worth considering as an alternative to the solution finally adopted, which two World Wars have accustomed us to regard as obvious, and even inevitable.

For despite the disappointments of the past two years, there still seemed much to be said for retaining Asquith as Prime Minister; and it is worth remembering that Balfour at the time, and Smuts later, were in favour of the arrangement. He was a good chairman of committee, whose virtues might indeed be displayed to greater effect under the new dispensation. He was still the dominant figure in the House of Commons, and retained the strong loyalties of most of his Party. And he was still on reasonably good terms with the higher ranks in the Services, although some at least of his retrospective popularity was probably the result of their experiences with his successor. If Asquith had remained Prime Minister, it can be argued that Lloyd George, as executive head of the war effort, might have been spared many of the political restrictions and embarrassments he encountered as head of the Government. An easier balance might have been struck between the claims of the rival Parties within the Coalition, and a Liberal leader might not have felt himself to so great an extent a captive of the Conservatives. 'It is no use being Prime Minister', Lloyd George told Lord Riddell in March 1918, 'unless you can do what you want to do. It is useless for me to say I can, because I can't. I have to make compromises all the time in order to conciliate different sections.'[1] The extent to which he had to do so was the result of events in December 1916.

This political constriction was felt most directly in Lloyd George's dealings with the army. As is well known, he had no confidence in Robertson as C.I.G.S. or in Haig as the British Commander-in-Chief in France; but he did not think himself strong enough to remove the former for over a year, and he never risked a direct challenge to the latter. The consequences were serious, for the military machine at home and at times for the Alliance. Had Asquith remained Prime Minister, it is arguable that better relations might have been established between the political and professional leaders, or that if, as seemed likely, this was impossible, the Government could have changed its principal adviser and commander without so grave a risk to its stability.

But when all this has been said, it remains difficult to see how the arrangement would have worked. The

[1] *Lord Riddell's War Diary* (1933), p. 317.

arguments in its favour, indeed, form merely a variant on those which have often been advanced, for different reasons, for the separation of the conduct of war from the conduct of politics. And whatever the attractions of such a solution at first sight, it has always foundered on its neglect of constitutional realities. It is not enough for a proposed system to take account of one level of authority and one aspect of government. It must—particularly as the effects of war become wider—comprehend all levels and aspects of government, which form an organic whole. As long as Parliamentary government by Departments retains its vitality, Ministers will remain responsible in war as they are in peace, and the Prime Minister will retain his full measure of executive authority. The implications of an alternative may indeed be seen on closer examination of the proposal made in 1916. For what in practice would have been the relations between the Prime Minister and a colleague who was nominally subordinate to him, and was always subject to his overriding authority, but who nevertheless was in day to day charge of the executive committee for running the war? Such a position might well have proved intolerable to both. It is quite possible for a wartime Prime Minister, in full possession of executive authority, to rely on a colleague for political support. Lloyd George found himself so obliged to Bonar Law in the House of Commons in 1917–18, and Mr Churchill to Mr Chamberlain within the Conservative Party in 1940. But the reverse does not follow. No Prime Minister in this century has acted as Parliamentary spokesman for a colleague with greater executive powers than himself. Cabinet government has demanded that whoever holds that power shall, by whatever means, assume the political consequences.

The same answer may be reached in another way. In the later stages of the First World War, the Cabinet system became increasingly dependent on a network of committees, which drew their authority from the centre of executive power. But if that power had been transferred to a body other than the Cabinet, how would the Cabinet itself, and its chairman, have held their authority? Whatever the safeguards devised, both would have found themselves increasingly elbowed off the stage, and the Prime Minister would have retained his Parliamentary authority only by involving himself in the machinery which derived from the War Committee. But for such a purpose he need not be Prime Minister at all. For Asquith to have filled the role for which he was apparently designed, he must have been identified so closely with Lloyd George's executive system that— unless he were to take the chair regularly himself, which was not the object of the arrangement—he would have become merely one of the Committee's directing Ministers: exactly as Neville Chamberlain became in 1940, and as there was no question of Asquith becoming in 1916.

Despite all of the later difficulties, it therefore seems as well that Asquith declined to serve the proposed arrangement, and that Lloyd George became Prime Minister in December 1916. It was then an obvious step for him to turn his proposed small War Committee into a War Cabinet. But by so doing he excluded the Service Ministers from the supreme organ, as he excluded all but one of the Departmental Ministers in the civil sphere.

The supervision of strategy was now entrusted to a small non-Departmental group, with the Prime Minister himself in active control. How was he to carry out this task, and what roles would be assigned to the various elements of the military machine?

There seems never to have been any serious intention of furnishing the Prime Minister with a regular committee of the War Cabinet for assistance in the direction of strategy, on the lines of the Ministerial Co-ordination and Defence Committees in the Second World War. A War Policy Committee was formed in June 1917 of Lloyd George, Curzon, Bonar Law, Milner, Smuts and the two Chiefs of Staff. But it was designed specifically to consider the strategy for that year alone, and came to an end by the early winter; and its nearest subsequent equivalent, the so-called X Committee of Lloyd George, Milner and Henry Wilson in the spring and summer of 1918, resembled a series of informal meetings by an inner group rather than a formal body. The absence of such a body may perhaps be attributed partly to the smallness of the War Cabinet itself. But it reflected in any case Lloyd George's preference for flexibility and informality in the difficult circumstances in which he worked; and in such matters, a Prime Minister's choice is decisive. For supreme strategic control does not demand the formal type of organization that is demanded by supreme economic control. The necessary co-ordination here takes place at a lower level, among the Staffs, and the Cabinet is free to exercise its responsibility in any form consonant with the personal and political conditions. As these will vary indefinitely, so will the shape and size of its organs; and the exact differences between them in different circumstances —the number and status of the Ministers included in each case—are not in fact particularly important in themselves. It is more relevant to put the question in another way: to turn from the Cabinet itself, and to seek to define the effect upon it in this sphere of the professional organization which supplies it with information and advice.

For it was the different uses made of this organization by the Cabinets of the First and Second World Wars that determined, in the event, the form of their control. In 1938, Mr Chamberlain remarked that the existence of a joint planning system, running up from the Service Departments to the Cabinet, had changed the whole problem of a War Cabinet since 1917; and it was indeed on the Chiefs of Staff's organization that the Cabinet's strategic authority came to rest in the war that followed. In 1917, on the contrary, that organization was only beginning to emerge along recognizable lines, and in circumstances that restricted and distorted its use. There was conflict, rather than co-operation, between the political and professional systems, with a consequent ambiguity in the Cabinet system itself. This conflict ceased, or at least eased significantly, in the course of 1918; and indeed in this respect the distinction between the two years is perhaps greater than has often been assumed. But the few months left before the Armistice did not suffice to reveal the implications for Cabinet government, and when the war ended they were still not clearly defined.

The great developments in the Staff system came in 1916 and 1917. They were most marked at first in the army. In the course of 1915, the inadequacy of the

General Staff became increasingly plain. The British army was now deployed in seven theatres of war—in France, Gallipoli, Salonika, Mesopotamia, Egypt, and East and West Africa; and while Mesopotamia lay beyond the purview of the C.I.G.S.,[1] he was in touch with no fewer than eleven Commanders-in-Chief. But the need to co-ordinate plans for the different campaigns was ill served by the machinery at the War Office. The complete subordination of the C.I.G.S. to the Secretary of State, and the consequent limits to the powers of the Staff, had unfortunate results. Central planning was feeble and arbitrary; the Commanders-in-Chief were not furnished regularly with guidance or even with information; and their orders, issued by the Army Council as a body and not by the C.I.G.S., were subjected as a result to inordinate delay. Despite some improvement in detail in the later days of Wolfe Murray, it was thus an impoverished and diminished system that greeted his successor at the end of 1915. But the position then changed significantly. The new C.I.G.S., Sir William Robertson, came from headquarters in France, where he had observed the faults of the central machinery and had already submitted his comments upon them. On arriving at the War Office he at once proposed new arrangements, which Kitchener to his credit accepted generously and which were codified by Order in Council. As a result, the C.I.G.S. was restored to his earlier position of *ex officio* first professional member of the Army Council; he was made solely responsible for the promulgation of

[1] As did the Persian Gulf and the Sudan. But no campaign was contemplated in either of those areas.

orders to Commanders-in-Chief, and for communications between the Staff and other bodies, including the Cabinet; and the Staff itself was strengthened in quality and partly remodelled. Robertson indeed went farther. He wanted the C.I.G.S. to be responsible for supervising the conduct of operations 'in all theatres and possible theatres of war', and he recommended to the Cabinet that 'all the military forces of the Empire should constitute an Imperial Army'.[1] He failed in these attempts. But within stricter limits, he gained some real successes. In the first half of 1916, operations in Mesopotamia were brought by stages within the aegis of the General Staff; and in matters for which it was still not directly responsible, it found itself in practice, as time went by, consulted as a matter of course by the authorities concerned. With all its faults, a 'Great Headquarters', to use Robertson's phrase, had been formed at the seat of government, headed by an officer reporting daily to the civil authorities. Such a system did not obtain at the time in any other of the belligerents, and was adopted in France only in 1917. The effect was felt throughout the military system. 'The gradual improvement of our position on all fronts', the Deputy Director of Training and Staff Duties at the War Office remarked at the end of the war, 'has been due to the improvement in the Staff work. The personnel of our troops deteriorated while the Staff improved.'[2] This of course was due mainly to hard experience on the fronts themselves. But it was fostered,

[1] Field Marshal Sir William Robertson, *Soldiers and Statesmen*, vol. 1 (1926), pp. 173–4.
[2] Arthur J. Marder, *Portrait of An Admiral: The Life and Papers of Sir Herbert Richmond* (1952), p. 330.

and rendered more effective, by the improvements to the Staff work in London.

One consequence of Robertson's reforms was better liaison with the navy, although this still left a good deal to be desired. Reform in the Admiralty came in the course of 1917, mainly as a result of the failure to deal with the U-boat campaign. The inner circles of Government had been dissatisfied with the Department for some time. As Hankey wrote privately in 1916, 'It is no good. The Navy has completely lost the spirit of the offensive';[1] and a year later this feeling had spread far enough for the *Daily Mail*, now prepared to beard the Admirals as it had earlier bearded Kitchener, to suggest that a naval secretariat should be established in Downing Street independently of the Admiralty. But in the summer of 1917, the Prime Minister was able to claim a victory within the Admiralty itself. His insistence on the introduction of the convoy system, against professional advice, led to a series of changes over the next few months. The First Lord, Carson, was successfully removed to a non-Departmental seat in the War Cabinet; the First Sea Lord, Admiral Jellicoe, with powers redefined by Order in Council, became at last Chief of the Naval Staff; four months later, a Deputy First Sea Lord was created, to relieve his superior of detailed duties in planning and training; and at the end of the year, the Naval Staff itself was redesigned. Together with other changes to the Board, these measures brought the Admiralty more closely into line with its own needs and those of the Government; and its efficiency increased in the course of 1918.

[1] Loc. cit. p. 201.

The developments in the Service Staffs were of great value to the central staff, serving first the War Committee and then the War Cabinet, which itself developed fast from early in 1916. 'As an organization', Lord Hankey has recorded, '...the War Committee was a vast improvement on its predecessors. Joint memoranda were provided regularly by the General Staffs of the Admiralty and War Office....In the Secretariat we had learned a good deal. Team-work was everywhere much improved.'[1] The linch-pin of the system was Hankey himself. 'I tell you,' Balfour exclaimed to his niece one day after the war, striking his stick on the ground as he spoke, ' that without Hankey we should not have won the War!'[2] He was thinking of his later efflorescence, as Secretary to the War Cabinet, the Imperial War Cabinet and the Supreme War Council. But the genesis of those achievements lay in the secretariat to the early committees, which by the end of 1916 had made Hankey a master of his craft. Possessing a unique experience of the practice of strategic co-ordination, thoroughly familiar with the powers and susceptibilities of the different Staffs and Departments, he showed a peculiar flair for interpreting Lloyd George's intentions, and for moulding administration to the very shape of policy. The value of his organization to the strategic organization as a whole increased immensely when it became the basis for the new secretariat to the War Cabinet. The close interaction within that body of the military and civil sections fostered a growing co-ordination between the two sectors of

[1] Hankey, *Government Control in War*, p. 39.
[2] Dugdale, *Balfour*, vol. II, p. 242.

government themselves. If, for instance, the Services and the Foreign Office in this country have been kept in touch with each other, it is due very largely to the practice which Hankey established in the First World War. But that was only one example of the beneficent activities of the central staff, as it underpinned the ramifying structure of the Cabinet Committee system.

It may therefore be said that by 1918 the lines had been set along which the Service and the central Staffs were to develop over the next thirty years; and, particularly in view of the Service Ministers' exclusion from the Cabinet, this might have seemed to favour an increase in the authority of the professional heads. But this was not immediately so. Indeed, the reverse was the case. For while the Staff system was developing, the Chiefs of Staff throughout 1917 became increasingly embroiled with the Prime Minister. The foundations of their authority, in fact, were being strengthened while its use was in dispute. And in the course of the struggle, the Prime Minister was driven, in his efforts to circumvent his professional advisers, to foster some strange expedients with the machinery they controlled.

The first sign of the approaching conflict appeared before Lloyd George became Prime Minister. Robertson's reforms to the General Staff were necessary and beneficent. But their ready acceptance by the Cabinet owed more to personalities than to principle. For the new arrangement offered Ministers, weary of Kitchener but afraid to displace him, an excellent opportunity to clip his wings without incurring public odium; and the

Cabinet turned the more readily to the Chief of the Staff because he was an alternative to the Secretary of State. But when Kitchener was drowned, and Lloyd George took over the War Office, the personal situation changed again; and the new Secretary of State, who had concurred willingly enough in the restrictions placed upon his predecessor, found them excessively irksome when applied to himself. 'No statesman with any self-respect', he wrote to Asquith in June 1916, 'would consent to occupy office under the humiliating conditions to which poor Kitchener had been reduced during the last few months of his life.' He pleaded for the return of greater powers to the Minister, to give him that 'weight in the councils of the Allies' which he should possess.[1]

Lloyd George's argument was reasonable enough from the point of view of the Secretary of State; for the recent formal acceptance of the C.I.G.S. as the Government's principal military adviser was in fact to mark the start of the Service Ministers' decline. But a statesman may view the same subject in different ways from different positions. Mr Churchill, for instance, who early in 1940 voiced the Service Ministers' protest at the powers enjoyed by the Chiefs of Staff, steadily increased those powers once he became Prime Minister. But Lloyd George's attitude did not change on assuming the supreme office. On the contrary, it hardened. The reasons are well known. The Prime Minister was diametrically opposed to the strategy favoured by Robertson and Haig, and held a low opinion of their capacities and of those of Jellicoe at the Admiralty. An ardent Easterner,

[1] *War Memoirs of David Lloyd George*, vol. II (1933), p. 763.

he was confronted by as ardent Westerners: a convinced supporter of the convoy system, he had to contend with an adviser who thought that convoys were then impractical. It was not, as has sometimes been said, that Lloyd George condemned all soldiers and sailors, although it often seemed uncommonly like it. But he had formed a low opinion of the military and naval systems as schools for high command, he resented the strategy which he inherited, and he was determined to show the men responsible for it, and their political supporters, that he intended to be master.

Much ink has been spilt on the results. They form one of the most exciting series of episodes in recent British political history. Convinced—and with reason—that he alone could make victory possible, and obliged to balance for over a year on a political tightrope, Lloyd George employed to the full his flair for manœuvre and intrigue. His opponents countered, though not with equal zest or ability. The stakes, and the temperature, were high. Lloyd George himself, and even the moderate and balanced Milner, were ready at times to believe that the army leaders sought to take over the government. Their fears were almost certainly exaggerated; but they point a situation to which there was never a parallel in the Second World War. Indeed, we have only to envisage the fate of an official historian set to write the story of grand strategy in the First World War to realize how fortunate in this respect those of the Second have been.

This grave dispute was settled in the event by developments within the Alliance, which, in the First World War as in the Second, affected the form of the national system.

The process, however, was different in each case. In the Second World War, it was the need to set up a unified command in the field—in the Far East, at the end of 1941 —which led to the establishment of the Combined Chiefs of Staff, with profound effects thereafter on the Allied and the British organizations. In the First World War, the creation of a system of Allied control preceded the acceptance of the idea of a unified command in the field.[1] But the very absence of such a command placed a correspondingly greater strain on the system of control, with results which, again, affected the British system.

The greatest single architect of an Allied organization in the First World War was Lloyd George. He looked to an effective co-ordination of both plans—which meant a supreme Allied body—and operations—which meant a unified command in the field. In 1917, he tried to foster both processes. The issue of command came to the fore at once. In December 1916 the first Allied Command had been formed in Salonika, under the French General Sarrail. In January 1917 the question arose, in far more difficult circumstances, for the Western Front. The acceptance of Nivelle's plan of campaign convinced Lloyd George that the operations needed a unified command, and he was the more persuaded of its desirability from his opinion of Haig. But, as so often, his methods were unfortunate; and although he had his way in the end, it was at the cost of losing the confidence of the

[1] As cause and effect. I do not therefore count for this purpose the experiment in Salonika, which had no direct result elsewhere, or the temporary arrangement on the Western Front under General Nivelle, which retarded rather than developed the final acceptance of a unified command.

army leaders and of the King, and of creating an atmosphere thoroughly unfavourable to the further consideration of the issue.

When it arose again, it was moreover at a difficult time. The arrangement with Nivelle came to an end with his offensive; and the experience, involved as it was in the animosities and confusion of the French hierarchy, was not a happy one for the British. By the autumn of 1917, indeed, all responsible British authorities—including Lloyd George—had abandoned, if in some cases only superficially, the idea of a unified command in France. But this only concentrated the Prime Minister's attention the more closely upon the complementary object of a unified system of control. There was already a respectable history of British efforts in this direction. Kitchener had first proposed the formation of a co-ordinating body in January 1915; his proposals had been echoed in Cabinet in October; in November, such a body had been established in principle; and in January 1916 an advisory Committee to the Allied Governments had been approved, with a permanent secretariat based on that of the British War Cabinet. This Committee had met in March in Paris, attended by representatives of the eight Allies; there had been a tripartite meeting of Prime Ministers in December in Rome, attended by the British, the French and the Italians; and another Allied conference in February 1917 in Moscow, attended by the same three Powers and the Russians. In all of these developments, the British Government had played a leading part.

By the beginning of 1917, in fact, the conference habit

was firmly established, and in the first ten months of that year there were no fewer than eleven meetings between the British and the French. But the permanent organization, approved early in 1916, had meanwhile failed to mature. In October 1917 Lloyd George therefore proposed that it should be revived, and that an Allied Staff should be added to it, to advise the heads of Government on the Allied strategy. As he put it later in the year, the existing system only enabled separate commanders to 'sew...plans together'—and '*Stitching is not strategy*'.[1] The proposed Staff would thus serve both in lieu of a unified command in France, and the wider and complementary object of relating the plans for the Western Front to those of other theatres.

The opportunity soon came to put this scheme into effect. In November 1917, the Italians were defeated at Caporetto; and at the Rapallo Conference in December, Lloyd George gained consent to his proposal for the creation of an Allied Supreme War Council. This was to consist of France, Britain, Italy and the United States, with the other Allied Powers attached; it was to be attended by the Prime Minister and one other Minister —not necessarily always the same—from each of the four Governments; and it would dispose of a secretariat, and of a permanent Council of Military Representatives —established in the event at Versailles—with its own staff and with right of access to all information. Hankey was made Secretary to the Supreme War Council, and the secretariat was modelled on the lines of that serving the British War Cabinet.

[1] *War Memoirs of David Lloyd George*, vol. IV (1934), pp. 2397–8.

It was at this point that the Allied system impinged upon the system in London. For Lloyd George's persistent and serious disagreements with Robertson and Haig led him to make some curious claims for the British Military Representative at Versailles. The Prime Minister had already sought on occasions—by proposing that Smuts should be given a command in the Near East independent of the General Staff, and by calling for strategic memoranda from outside figures to be considered in the War Policy Committee of the War Cabinet —to circumvent his responsible advisers. The new Allied body now seemed to provide him with more effective means to that end. While the other Allies identified their representatives, either in person or by responsibility, with the Chiefs of Staff of their armies, the British member of the Council was Henry Wilson, who was directed to report to the Prime Minister 'and', as Wilson himself gleefully recorded, 'not to anyone else'.[1] So much, Lloyd George thought, for Robertson. The next move followed soon. In February 1918 the Prime Minister proposed—and it was an excellent idea in itself—the creation of an Allied reserve for the Western Front. But since there was no Allied commander to command it, he suggested that it should be placed at the disposal of an Executive Board at Versailles, responsible to the Supreme War Council and almost identical in its composition with the Council of Military Representatives. So much for Haig.

Both of these moves achieved their objects, one di-

---

[1] Major-General Sir C. E. Callwell, *Field-Marshal Sir Henry Wilson, His Life and Diaries*, vol. II (1927), p. 31.

rectly, the other indirectly. The powers given to Wilson were clearly designed to force Robertson's hand; and after a confused and unedifying struggle at the end of 1917, Lloyd George gained the desired result. Robertson was dismissed, and in February 1918 Wilson himself became C.I.G.S. It is interesting to observe that he at once changed his mind about the British representative at Versailles. His successors in that post, Sir Henry Rawlinson and General Sackville-West, found themselves brought firmly under the aegis of the War Office; and the pattern of command which Wilson had opposed so loquaciously in 1917 was consolidated, by his own efforts, in the spring of the following year.

Meanwhile, the attempt to establish a General Reserve was leading to fresh suggestions for a co-ordinating authority on the Western Front itself. Various arrangements were proposed, which the German offensive overtook. At the Doullens Conference in March, Milner committed the British Government to recognizing Foch as the co-ordinator 'of the Allies about Amiens' in the current operations. But this formula soon proved inadequate, and in April, after some intervening steps, Foch was created 'General-in-Chief of the Allied Forces in France'.

Thus, by a devious route, the Allies acquired an organ of supreme control and a unified command on the most important front.[1] Two consequences followed in London. First, the C.I.G.S. confirmed his professional authority

[1] In the atmosphere engendered by this achievement, the French suggested in May 1918 that unified command should be applied also to the Allied Fleets in the Mediterranean, and that Jellicoe should fill the post.

in the Allied as in the national system, although only in the course of a process designed at first with the opposite purpose. But secondly, this confirmation of his authority was not accompanied by an increase in his power. On the contrary, once again a development which in the long run was to strengthen his position failed in the short run to have that effect. For Wilson as C.I.G.S. was peculiarly Lloyd George's nominee, and it was the Prime Minister who benefited most from the changes that had been made. Emerging victorious from the long struggle with Robertson, Lloyd George was in no mood to stand for independence from his professional adviser. In April 1918, he reinforced his authority by sending Milner, the strongest and one of the closest of his colleagues, to the War Office as Secretary of State; and from May, when he triumphed in the Maurice Debate, his political supremacy was at last ensured. The C.I.G.S. was now in harness with a more powerful team than his predecessor; and when in the spring and summer of 1918 the X Committee handled affairs for the War Cabinet,[1] it was the politicians and not the soldier who were effectively in control.

The Council of Military Representatives was only one of the subordinate organs which the Supreme War Council developed in the final year of the war. It also disposed of an Allied Naval Council in London, of an Allied Transportation Council at Versailles, and on the economic side of a whole network of Councils, Commissions, Committees and Executives. Lord Hankey has shown the details, in a chart of the organization for

[1] See p. 80 above.

November 1918.[1] The story of its development belongs to the history of Allied control, rather than to that of Cabinet government in this country. So too does the story of the Imperial organization at this stage, which again was the child of Lloyd George's imagination. Until his accession to power, the Dominion Governments had been represented in the Cabinet system only by occasional attendance on the part of visiting Ministers, and in the case of Canada alone by a permanent representative with access to meetings of the Committee of Imperial Defence. But in December 1916 the new Prime Minister invited the Dominions to attend a series of 'special and continuous' meetings of the War Cabinet, and in the event three sessions were held, one in 1917 and two in 1918. Neither the Dominion Governments nor the War Cabinet wished these meetings to be held as meetings of the British body; and two new organs were accordingly created, the Imperial War Cabinet, composed of Cabinet Ministers selected from the British and Dominion Governments, and a complementary Imperial War Conference, consisting of Ministers and officials under the chairmanship of the Colonial Secretary.

The Imperial War Cabinet, in Sir Winston Churchill's words, 'centred in a single executive the world-spread resources of the British Monarchy'.[2] But it did so only in the periods—never exceeding three months—for which it was summoned, and, unlike the Supreme War Council with its standing bodies, thus served to focus the work of

---

[1] The Rt Hon. Lord Hankey, *Diplomacy by Conference* (1946), p. 10.
[2] *The World Crisis, 1916–18, Part I* (1927), p. 257.

existing organs rather than to incorporate them in a new structure. But both permanent and temporary organizations had a similar effect on the system in London. 'What we really want to know', Balfour wrote in December 1917, 'is whether...the combined military, economic and political "squeeze" which the Allies will be able to exercise upon the Central Powers is greater than the "squeeze" which the Central Powers can exercise upon the Allies.'[1] This was a conception of total war, which administrative systems, developed along lines very different from each other, were striving with limited experience and effect to approach. It demanded the rationalization of national efforts, and their combination in an international effort; and the British system, already more highly developed than those of the other Allies, formed in this process the basis for a development which in turn affected itself.[2] In 1914 it had still been true to say, though it was becoming less so, that 'the business of everybody is the business of nobody'.[3] By 1919, that conception had disappeared.

The administrative process, so notably advanced at the end of 1916, accordingly continued with increasing force in the last year of the war. Two more Ministries—Air and Propaganda—and two Departments—Mines and Overseas Trade—were created; and, at the centre, the Cabinet began to assemble various groups of ad-

[1] Dugdale, *Balfour*, vol. II, p. 253.

[2] '...the new Allied principle did not override or replace the national organizations—it penetrated them.' J. A. Salter, *Allied Shipping Control, An Experiment in International Administration* (1921), p. 251.

[3] T. B. Macaulay, *Historical Essays Contributed to the Edinburgh Review:* review of Hallam's *Constitutional History* (September 1828).

ministrative problems under a number of heads, each the concern of a standing committee. The War Priorities Committee, chronologically the first of these bodies,[1] developed an elaborate organization, culminating in seventeen sub-Committees grouped under four inter-mediate organs. In the course of 1918, the War Cabinet also set up another four permanent committees, the Eastern, Economic Defence and Development, Home Affairs, and Demobilization Committees; and there were others again which, in the words of the War Cabinet Report for that year, 'met so frequently and so continu-ously as to fall almost into the category of Standing Committees'.[2] Of these, a notable example was the Army and Navy Pay Committee. All of the standing bodies were given wide powers, under a Minister of the War Cabinet. All were inter-Departmental, and relied upon the War Cabinet's secretariat to handle their business with the Departments. In selected fields and for selected purposes, a new link was being forged in the chain of executive responsibility.

This system of permanent committees was in its in-fancy at the end of the war. It was spread unevenly over different areas; relations varied greatly between the committees and the Departments, and between the War Cabinet Ministers, their committees and the sub-committees; and the hierarchy itself was incomplete. In particular, there was no co-ordinating committee, such as was found necessary in the Second World War, to supervise the work of the rest throughout the civil sphere.

[1] See p. 75 above.
[2] Cmd. 325 (1919), p. 5.

But the essential characteristics of a novel type of war system were present, emerging from an older system which had not been destroyed in the process. The Departmental organization had been revised and extended; links had been established between the Departments, not by means of superior Departments, but by Cabinet committees; and those committees were being developed to serve a small War Cabinet, the sole repository of executive power. Informing this system was the personal authority of the Prime Minister, at last politically secure and correspondingly more free to give a fresh impulse to the higher direction. What courses that impulse might have taken it is hard to guess. Lloyd George was at once a creative and a destructive force. A superb organizer for war, he could build new administrative structures, and by his personal authority could influence the work in great areas of government. He could also drive his colleagues and subordinates to disillusion and resentment, and impair his own achievements by interference or distrust. These habits seemed to be growing on him towards the end of the war. On the other hand, the forces that had encouraged his less estimable qualities were themselves on the decline. A more favourable atmosphere was developing in the last six months of 1918. What, we may ask, might have been the result had the war continued into the following year? Is it absurd to suggest that the settlement of the political difficulties, which had hitherto had so marked an effect on the central organization, might have been followed by an improvement in its working, and that as the quarrels between the Prime Minister and his Service advisers declined, as

Allied co-operation increased, and as the permanent committees of Cabinet consolidated their authority, a more stable and effective system might at last have been secured? As it was, the process was cut short. The war ended with vivid memories of personal and administrative conflict. And when study and criticism came to play upon its last two years, it was on the struggles of a pioneering period that they fastened, rather than on the implications of a last, short period of promise.

CHAPTER IV

CONSOLIDATION, REARMA-MENT AND THE TEST OF THE SECOND WORLD WAR, 1919–40

TOWARDS the end of the First World War, there was a good deal of unease in Whitehall at the state of the machinery of government. The unavoidable improvisations of an increasingly crowded and critical period had produced many anomalies and distortions. At the same time, it was recognized that the mould of the pre-war system had been shattered. In 1917, a committee was accordingly appointed, under Lord Haldane, to investigate the position as a whole; and in the following year it produced its proposals. They were not, however, destined to have much effect. As Lord Salter has remarked, the Haldane Report has 'been used more by the political student than the practical statesman'.[1] Envisaging a further radical redistribution of Departmental powers, and the continuation of a small Cabinet which bore little relation to normal political conditions, it was indeed inherently unlikely to appeal to officials or to Ministers involved in the administrative and political aftermath of war. But if the recommendations had little positive effect on government as a whole, they had a certain negative effect on the structure of the organization for defence.

[1] Arthur Salter, *Personality in Politics: Studies of Contemporary Statesmen* (1947), p. 118.

The Committee's observations on this head were brief, and at first sight even cursory. They occupied half a page of the report, and were confined to a bald approval of the Staff system in the Services, and of the Committee of Imperial Defence as the central co-ordinating body. But this unadorned support of existing arrangements was more important than it might have seemed; for it was given, with authority, at a time when proposals for radical change were in the air, and could be invoked the more readily for its conservatism because much of the rest of the report had proved itself radical.

The general tenor of the proposals for change was for a more formal association between the Services. The objects were not always the same. Some reformers envisaged a single inter-Service Staff, some a single agent of supply for the forces, some a Ministry of Defence. But whatever the differences between the solutions proposed, or indeed between the arguments advanced, they all showed a strong feeling for integration as such, which was expressed at intervals in Parliament and in the Press.

Much of this feeling arose from the fact that there was now a third Service—a phenomenon unique to this country for some years. Its creation in 1918 was the outcome of one of the bitterest struggles within the Government during the First World War. By August 1917, the War Cabinet had come to the conclusion that the growing size of the air arm demanded new arrangements for its control. The existing machinery was clumsy. Air policy and operations were in the hands of the Board of Admiralty and the Army Council, on each of which expert opinion was now represented; production and supply in those of the Ministry of Munitions; and co-ordination between the Departments and with the Cabinet in those of successive Air Boards, furnished with their own expert committees. It was difficult to settle priorities, and impossible to settle policy, when two Services were interested in the same weapon for largely different ends; while the Air Boards, in their advisory capacities, displayed many of the unsatisfactory features that had plagued the earlier central advisory committees. In the autumn of 1917, the War Cabinet therefore did as it had done in other not dissimilar cases, and decided to examine the possibility of creating a new Department. General Smuts was put in charge of an exploratory Air Organization Committee, while a temporary Air Policy Committee was formed, with strong powers, to replace the Air Board. Smuts' Committee moved fast. In December 1917, an Air Council was appointed; in January 1918, a Secretary of State for Air presiding over an Air Ministry;[1] and in April, the existing air forces were combined in the Royal Air Force.

The new Service was formed in the teeth of opposition from its elder sisters, particularly from the navy; and it felt itself from the start something of a Cinderella—with a Cinderella's future. Naturally independent from the conditions of its birth, it was the more determined to remain so from the knowledge that it might be on the verge of a great expansion. In the course of the war, over 58,000 aircraft were produced, the greater proportion in

---

[1] For his various changes of title in practice in the early days, see Viscount Templewood, *Empire of the Air* (1957), p. 49.

the last eighteen months. But the programme for 1919 was on a much grander scale than its predecessor. At the Armistice, the outstanding contracts for the aircraft industry in the Ministry of Munitions amounted to some £165 million—over half its total commitments for all purposes at that date. In the light of this production, and of the potentialities of the new weapon, opinion on the Air Council was swinging, even in 1918, towards its use primarily as an independent force. The swing continued after the war, within the Ministry and, despite continued fierce opposition, in the Committee of Imperial Defence; and in the first half of the twenties, a new doctrine of air power began to emerge. Here then was a new Service, with its own claims and its own character, bringing much that was new to the problems of national defence. For strategic thought in the Air Staff was something different from that in the Naval and General Staffs. It moved, with possibilities as yet unknown, towards different objects, at a different pace, and in a different dimension. Its practitioners were conscious that they inhabited a world far removed in many ways from that of the soldier or the sailor; and they soon introduced into strategic planning techniques and modes of thought that were not easily assimilated. The older Services, for their part, challenged many of the claims for a method of warfare of which there was no experience, and which demanded its proportion of the limited funds available to defence as a whole. The debate was long and stormy, and was echoed in public, attracting passions similar to those roused earlier by the controversies of the 'blue-water' school. It continued, varying its forms, into the Second World

War; and indeed the debt that is owed to the Chiefs of Staff in handling the problem at that time, and particularly to Air Marshal Portal as Chief of the Air Staff, can be appreciated only against the background of the inter-war years.

This new and undigested element was introduced into planning at the beginning of a decade when the international prospects for defence were uncertain. The Cabinet's 'ten-year rule' began to operate in a period when the shape of strategy was in any case hard to foresee. There was no one obvious potential enemy or alliance of enemies, and planning accordingly became largely a matter of long-term speculation—an exercise whose decline has often been deplored when short-term issues occupy the foreground, but which is itself of limited value when such issues do not exist. In these conditions, there was inevitably a tendency for the three Services to plan along different lines: according to some critics, the divergencies went dangerously far. The navy, it was said, was much concerned with the Pacific; the army with India and the Near East as well as with Europe; the air force with Europe alone. The remedy, it seemed to many, was to integrate the Staffs in a single machine, which would force them to adopt common standards and objects.

Other critics fastened on the implications for supply. The forces formed potentially the biggest customer of industry in the country, and many of their demands upon it were broadly of the same character. They should not therefore be left to compete, but should combine their programmes into a coherent whole, itself worked out on the basis of a coherent strategic design. For this purpose the experience of the war should be acknowledged in peace, and a single agency of supply should be created, preferably in the form of a Department on the analogy of the wartime Ministry of Munitions.

Such proposals reached a natural climax in the demand for a Ministry of Defence, under a Minister superior to the existing Service Ministers. In addition to the advantages claimed for a single Staff and a single agent of supply, there were said to be strictly administrative merits in such an organization. The War Cabinet had found it necessary to handle the problems of demobilization and of pay for the forces by means of permanent and semi-permanent Committees.[1] Why not handle all matters affecting personnel in future through the more familiar medium of a Department? Some advocates of the scheme called attention to Mr Churchill's remark, when acting for a short time as simultaneously Secretary of State for War and for Air, that he found himself much assisted thereby in handling questions common to both Services. Others stressed (though, as the findings of the Weir and May Committees showed, without foundation) an anticipated reduction in expense as well as the anticipated increase in efficiency.

The Government, however, was not impressed by these proposals, on the various occasions on which they were raised in the twenties and early thirties. It was opposed particularly strongly to the idea of a Ministry of Defence, which seemed to it to confuse problems of administration with those of policy, and to seek to combine in one institution processes of government which

[1] See p. 97 above.

were essentially separate from each other. Nor did formal integration seem relevant to any one of those processes. While some administrative questions were common to all Services, many more were not; and the same applied to questions of supply. The Weir (initially the Mond) Committee, set up to consider an amalgamation of services common to the forces, returned an explicit answer in 1926. '. . . The amalgamation of the common services of the three Departments', it pronounced, 'is not advisable; and we doubt if any substantial economies would thereby be effected.'[1] This verdict can scarcely be gainsaid in the circumstances in which it was given, and to which, as the Committee was careful to point out, it referred. Even when a Ministry of Supply was eventually formed, on the eve of the Second World War, it proved undesirable to combine supply for the navy with that for the other two Services; and in a period of retrenchment there can be little doubt that the Government was right to foster co-ordination in this field by more modest and flexible methods.

But the most forcible arguments against formal integration in defence were those in favour of the existing system for determining policy. In the first place, it seemed pointless to try to overcome differences between separate Staffs by imposing an artificial unity upon them. On the contrary, the differences were more likely to be aggravated than reduced thereby. Defence must obviously be viewed as a whole. But this would not be facilitated by ignoring the identities of the parts. The Service Staffs, as Lord Haldane observed at the time,

[1] Cmd. 2649 (1926), p. 5.

'should meet and consult, but they will consult all the better if they come as grown intelligences'.[1]

And if a single Staff was not the instrument best calculated to offer professional advice, a Ministry of Defence seemed irrelevant to the purposes for which advice was offered. 'The most difficult and important problems of all', the Service Ministers had informed Balfour at the beginning of the century, were 'those which are neither purely naval nor purely military, nor purely naval and military combined, but which may be described as naval, military and political.'[2] A Ministry of the kind envisaged would add nothing to the means available for dealing with such problems. The real need was rather, as it had been earlier, to ensure that the Cabinet's organization functioned effectively. It was the Cabinet to which the Staffs must report, and which must provide the context for their deliberations; and the essential agent in this exchange was the Committee of Imperial Defence, operating, under the aegis of the Prime Minister, with an authority and with functions inevitably different from those of a Department under another Minister in formal control of the defence system.

And lastly, the critics of the existing system seemed to have forgotten its historical background. The Committee of Imperial Defence had evolved in response to the needs of an imperial and maritime strategy; and while the Empire was being transformed in part into a Commonwealth, and sea power had increasingly to take account of the air, the fundamental postulates of control remained

[1] Maurice, *Haldane*, vol. II, p. 79.
[2] See p. 28 above.

the same. The central instrument must accord with a subtle and indirect system of power: with a group of nations whose members stood in various relations to the central member, and with a flexible and pragmatic form of warfare calling for the co-operation rather than the integration of the different arms. A Ministry of Defence was unlikely to improve for these purposes on the Committee of Imperial Defence. It would confuse, to an unknown extent, the relations between the British Cabinet and other Commonwealth Governments. It would transfer to a Department, again to an unknown extent, functions whose performance had hitherto fallen entirely to a committee under the Prime Minister. And in substituting, in whatever degree, the authority of a Department for that of an advisory committee, it would disturb the pattern of existing Departmental responsibilities to Parliament. The force of these arguments may indeed be measured by the arrangements adopted in the years immediately following the Second World War—still similar in their strategic assumptions to the last stage of that conflict—in which there has been a Minister of Defence co-ordinating the affairs of three Services, but one who has derived his authority not so much from his Department—which as an administrative organ has been derisory—as from the fact that he has been responsible for a network of defence committees housed within its walls.

It was accordingly on the existing structure of the Committee of Imperial Defence that Governments decided to build in the twenties and early thirties. The Committee itself was resuscitated in principle in November 1919,

after its wartime hibernation within the War Committees and the War Cabinet. But there proved no occasion
for it to meet until the summer of 1920, and meanwhile
various of its sub-Committees—Oversea Defence, defence of the Home Ports, Departmental Co-ordination—
undertook the necessary detailed work. When the main
Committee met, moreover, it was to sanction a new, and
interesting, delegation of its powers. For it then decided
to set up a Standing Defence sub-Committee, consisting
of the Prime Minister, the Chiefs of Staff of the Services,
a few senior Departmental officials, and representatives
from the Dominions when possible, to consider questions
of policy referred to it by the Committee of Imperial
Defence; and that body in practice took over the work of
its parent for the next two to three years. The Prime
Minister, who found himself unable to attend regularly,
soon delegated his chairmanship to a colleague; and
Lloyd George and Bonar Law entrusted the work to
Balfour and Salisbury respectively.

Although this development may not have been clearly
planned or its implications foreseen, it showed—as had
been shown in the last few years before the war—that the
full Committee of Imperial Defence was too unwieldy for
the vital task of strategic planning; and, combined with
the experience of an *ad hoc* committee of the Chiefs of
Staff in the Chanak crisis of 1922, it pointed the way to an
important development in the following year. In 1923,
a sub-Committee on National and Imperial Defence was
set up, under Lord Salisbury, to review the central
machinery. It proposed in its report that the three Chiefs
of Staff should form their own standing committee,

under the chairmanship of the Prime Minister or his deputy, to consider and investigate, whether by reference or on their own initiative, the problems of Imperial defence and of co-ordination between the Services. In a phrase which has often been quoted, the aim was to provide a body with 'an individual and collective responsibility for advising on defence policy as a whole,... constituting, as it were, a Super-Chief of a War Staff in Commission'.[1]

The Chiefs of Staff soon formed their central staffs for planning and intelligence, to which they later added a sub-Committee of Deputy Chiefs of Staff to relieve them of the less important work. They soon came to sit, also, as a purely professional body, seldom attended by the Prime Minister or his deputy. With their creation, the purely military sector of defence planning had indeed been settled on a satisfactory basis. But Governments were now well aware that national defence involved far more than that sector alone. Robertson had estimated, as C.I.G.S. in the First World War, that he was responsible for no more than 25 per cent of the war effort; for, as General Ismay put it in 1938, the armed forces were only the 'cutting edge of a defence mechanism which includes every single Department of State'.[2] It was indeed one of the strongest arguments for the Committee system that it offered a reasonable means of devising and

[1] Cmd. 2029 (1924), p. 18. There would seem to be some causal connexion between this development and the experience of the Standing Defence sub-Committee, since the latter was suppressed by the instrument that created the Chiefs of Staff sub-Committee (loc. cit. p. 18).

[2] Major-General H. L. Ismay, 'The Machinery of the Committee of Imperial Defence', in *Journal of the Royal United Service Institution*, vol. LXXXIV (1939), p. 247.

controlling such a mechanism; and it was on the links between the military and civil parts that attention fastened largely in the period between the wars.

From the start, the process was brought within the aegis of the Committee of Imperial Defence; and indeed its success in this supervisory, co-ordinating capacity was the complement to its failure as an organ of strategic planning. In 1920, as a first step, it formed a sub-Committee to consider the question of national service in a future war. As a result, a Standing inter-Departmental Committee was set up which, in 1924, became the sub-Committee on Manpower, under the chairmanship of the President of the Board of Trade. Another important step was taken in the same year, with the formation of a Committee of Principal Supply Officers, which three years later was confirmed in a slightly altered form and charged with the duty of planning industrial mobilization for war. This organization soon expanded, along lines similar to those of the parent body. It met only occasionally, under the chairmanship of the President of the Board of Trade, and delegated its duties to a Supply Board, concerned with industrial capacity, and to a Board of Trade Supply Organization, concerned with raw materials. They in turn proliferated a chain of committees and sub-committees, so that a network of inter-Departmental advisory bodies covered in theory the field of production and supply.

Meanwhile, the older organs of the Committee of Imperial Defence, inherited from before the war, continued their work in association with the new machinery. By the later twenties, the Committee's responsibilities could be divided into five main heads—strategic planning (handled by the Chiefs of Staff and their subordinates), organization for war (handled in the main by the older sub-Committees), manpower (the concern of the Manpower sub-Committee), supply (handled by the Principal Supply Officers' organization), and miscellaneous (including research, falling mainly to the Chiefs of Staff and the Principal Supply Officers). The strength of this complex and extensive system lay in the fact that it covered the whole range of administrative instruments without detracting from their executive responsibilities. The members of the central committees, at whatever level, retained without exception their individual allegiances to a Service or a Department. The officers and officials who planned belonged to the institutions which had to execute. Ministers, for their part, continued to be personally responsible to Parliament. They sat, as before, in a Cabinet of normal peacetime dimensions, itself functioning in the traditional ways and possessing its traditional collective responsibility. But at the same time they and their organizations were represented on a single advisory organization for defence, which now concerned itself, if with differing degrees of success, in every aspect of the subject. As Mr Baldwin told the House of Commons in 1928, only one out of more than fifty sub-Committees of the Committee of Imperial Defence was confined to representatives of the Services alone, and ninety-five of the last hundred items of business had involved one or more of the civil Departments.

This system was tested by events from 1935 to 1939. In November 1934, the Committee of Imperial Defence directed those of its bodies concerned with the defence of the United Kingdom to plan on the assumption of a possible war with Germany within five years. In March 1935, the Government issued the first of a series of White Papers on Defence. These two acts marked the start of a short but increasingly crowded period, very different from that of the preceding fifteen years, whose conditions naturally affected the work, and the shape, of the central machinery.

Three main tasks faced the Government in the middle and later thirties: to plan a reasonable strategy for war; to provide the means for its execution; and to design an effective system of direction, in a time of armed peace, for a conflict which might come suddenly and, as it was believed, with immediate ferocity. The machinery for the first of these tasks proved in general satisfactory. The Chiefs of Staff's hierarchy was well fitted to consider problems of strategy which became increasingly specific; and they, and the older group of sub-Committees concerned with domestic defence and departmental co-ordination, were able to absorb without undue difficulty the new organization for civil defence against air raids.

It was far less easy to provide, or even to plan for, the necessary means. The two great questions here were manpower and supply. The former remained the business of the Manpower sub-Committee, which made some progress with its plans for conscription on the outbreak of war. But in fact these were largely negative in conception. For the Committee's work was restricted to the armed forces alone, and Governments showed themselves notably shy of tackling the admittedly speculative and dangerous problems affecting the national manpower as a whole. In 1937, a proposal for a National Register was abruptly refused; and preparations for conscription accordingly centred on the prevention of indiscriminate enlistment rather than on the best positive use of all available resources.

Supply raised more complex problems than manpower, if only because they could not be left to the outbreak of war. The conditions for the rearmament programme differed both from those of 1916–18, when it was a matter of devising the best means to attain an obvious end, and from those of the twenties, when all that was needed was to protect the foundations of a structure that was not itself required. Perhaps the closest parallel was to be found in the experience of 1914–16, when the proportions of industrial mobilization were changing within an economy not yet fully geared to war. But this parallel was itself inexact; for on this occasion a similar problem had to be tackled in peace, and by a generation more conscious of the economic and administrative issues involved.

Until the last few months before the war, the burden fell almost entirely on the Principal Supply Officers and their subordinates; who, as they stood, were not well fitted to endure it. Their organization showed two weaknesses in particular in the new conditions. Developed as an instrument for designing a war potential, it was not so well equipped to produce a policy for remedying current deficiencies; and, given a policy of this immediate nature, it was not well suited to carry it out. Neither weakness was entirely the fault of the Principal Supply Officers themselves. As early as 1926 they had envisaged an organization for war, in which the supply of raw materials would become the business of a Ministry of Material Resources, while the responsibility for devising policy would fall to a Ministerial Priority Committee. If those two measures had been adopted early in the course of the rearmament programme, they might have mitigated some of the difficulties it encountered; although these were bound in any case to be formidable, in the industrial conditions created by the 'ten-year rule' as applied from 1929 to 1933. But it is doubtful if, even so, the measures would have proved enough by themselves. For, admirable though it was as far as it went, the scheme of 1926 had two defects. It looked to the outbreak of war rather than to a prior period of rearmament, and thus tended to gloss over the preliminaries in its concentration on the final step; and it was vague—and deliberately so—on the machinery to be devised for production, as distinct from that for the supply of raw materials.

It was on this gap that criticism fastened most strongly during the four years before the Second World War. Much of that criticism was confused, and invited the comments it received on the many discrepancies between the arguments advanced. But they were at one in deploring a system of executive co-ordination purely by committee, and the lack of a single Minister responsible to Parliament for the programme as a whole. The Government, for its part, took the line that the creation of a Ministry of Supply might retard rather than hasten the fulfilment of the programme: by disturbing the inadequate staff available, by posing awkward questions of responsibility for the new Ministry in peacetime conditions, and by destroying the traditional structure of the Service Departments, in which the providers and the users of weapons were intimately associated within the same organization.

These arguments sounded not unreasonable in the early stages of rearmament. But as it progressed, most of them lost their force. Nor in fact did the existing system prove satisfactory even in the earlier stages of the programme. In 1935, the Supply Board—on which most of the work then fell—was granted extra staff and a more effective direction; and thus armed managed, as the Treasury noted with some apprehension, to extend its activities 'rather beyond the advisory capacity of the Committee of Imperial Defence into a more executive sphere'.[1] But the penetration remained modest. The members of the staff of the central body found themselves increasingly involved in their separate Departmental duties; and executive co-ordination was in any case limited by the inadequacies of the machinery for producing policy.

For both the pressure and the restrictions on the Principal Supply Officers' organization were increased by the confusion and inadequacy at a higher level. The Ministerial Priority Committee, advocated and approved in principle in the twenties, did not emerge. Instead, a series of Ministerial bodies was set up with rather different and less effective functions. For the planning and supervision of the rearmament programme

[1] Quoted in J. D. Scott and Richard Hughes, *The Administration of War Production* (1955), p. 56.

soon became involved in the complementary but essentially distinct business of strategic planning, with a consequent ambiguity in the organization for both. In the autumn of 1933, the Committee of Imperial Defence decided to set up a Defence Requirements sub-Committee, consisting of the Chiefs of Staff and Departmental officials, to report on various problems affecting disarmament. This was later strengthened by some Ministerial members, and in July 1935, in the new conditions set by the rearmament programme, it was formally reconstituted as the Defence Policy Requirements sub-Committee, under the chairmanship of the President of the Board of Trade. But a few months later, when the Mediterranean crisis came to a head, this body found itself placed in charge of all immediate arrangements for defence. The Prime Minister took the chair, membership became that of an inner circle of the Committee of Imperial Defence, and the sub-Committee in practice replaced its parent rather as the Standing Defence sub-Committee had done in the early twenties.[1] When the crisis ended, it reverted to its earlier task. But the Chiefs of Staff, who had welcomed its operations as a small directing body on behalf of the Cabinet, now wished to see such a body established as a permanent feature of government; and in January 1937, the Prime Minister accordingly agreed to set up for this purpose a Defence Plans (Policy) sub-Committee, distinct from the Defence Policy Requirements sub-Committee, and consisting exclusively of senior and Service Ministers with himself or a deputy in the chair. Early in 1937, there were thus

[1] See p. 109 above.

three organs of Cabinet concerned with defence policy —the Committee of Imperial Defence, and its two sub-Committees—'all', in Lord Hankey's words at the time, 'more or less independent of one another, all dealing with defence questions without very definite lines of demarcation'.[1] The results, not unnaturally, were confusing, to the rest of the organization for defence and to the three Ministerial Committees themselves. Towards the end of the year, the position was therefore clarified. The remedy was found, once more, in the Committee of Imperial Defence itself, which having spawned the two sub-Committees was now required to reabsorb them. Their meetings, held with distinct membership in each case and on regular and distinct occasions, became meetings of the main Committee; and, thus presenting again a simple and familiar appearance to the outside world, they found it easier to regulate their duties under the name and aegis of the parent body.

The Committee of Imperial Defence had thus again shown its value as a flexible agent of government. But it did not thereby solve the problems of supply which had partly occasioned the process, and to which an answer was delayed until the eve of war. The process also underlined a fact that had been becoming more obvious for some time. The Prime Minister himself could no longer hope to supervise the detailed work of the Committee in person. The practice of the post-war years, whereby he had appointed a deputy, had latterly been discontinued. Macdonald and Baldwin in the middle twenties, following the precedent set by Lloyd George and Bonar Law

[1] Scott and Hughes, loc. cit. p. 65.

with Balfour and Salisbury, had entrusted normal super-vision of the Committee to Haldane and Curzon respect-ively. But when Curzon died in 1925—and despite the recent recommendation of the Salisbury Committee that a deputy should be maintained—Baldwin took over this duty himself; and Macdonald did likewise from 1929 to 1935. At the beginning of 1936, however, Baldwin decided that a deputy was once more necessary, and on this occasion with full-time responsibilities and a distinct Ministerial status. In February, he accordingly an-nounced the appointment of Sir Thomas Inskip as Minister for the Co-ordination of Defence. The duties and powers of the new Minister were defined by the system he joined. He became deputy chairman to the Prime Minister on the Committee of Imperial Defence, the Chiefs of Staff sub-Committee, and the sub-Com-mittees—as they still were then—of Defence Policy Requirements and Defence Plans (Policy); and, from 1938, he was chairman of the Manpower sub-Commit-tee. He thus operated exclusively within the central organization, as the agent of the Prime Minister on bodies which the latter could not supervise in detail himself. There was no suggestion by the Government that he should assume executive powers over any com-bination of Departments. He was merely designed, as his title made clear, to strengthen the Prime Minister's control of a co-ordinating advisory system.

So matters stood when the Munich crisis arose in the second half of 1938. Its experience produced further developments to the central system. The narrow avoidance of war, and the immediate dangers ahead, convinced all authorities that they must adopt, so far as seemed possible, a preparatory organization for war. Time was now of the essence. Hostilities might begin within a year. The whole system was therefore tightened. Preparations were made for closer links with the representatives of the Dominions. A Minister for Civil Defence and Voluntary Service was created, and placed as a deputy in this sphere to the Minister for the Co-ordination of Defence. The Manpower sub-Committee was strengthened, and arrangements were made to incorporate a Department of National Service within the Ministry of Labour. Plans were prepared to establish other Ministries when war came—Home Security (to be incorporated in the Home Office), Economic Warfare, Information, Food, and Shipping—as the experience of the previous war had shown to be necessary.[1] And the machinery for supply was at last improved both for policy and for execution. In April 1939, the long-advocated Ministerial Priority Committee was formed, to provide a more powerful control at the point of policy where it was needed; and in August, after a last spirited debate, the Government consented to establish a Ministry of Supply. Thus, as had happened in several instances in the First World War and was to happen again in the Second, inadequate executive co-ordination by a committee led to the creation of a fresh Department—a secondary process, as it were, within the evolution of the Committee system itself.

[1] In the event, the Ministries of National Service, Home Security, Economic Warfare, Information, and Food were set up in September 1939, and Shipping in October.

The crisis also raised again, and now more urgently, the question of an effective directing body at the summit. Four methods of control by a Cabinet system could be envisaged from past experience, according to the nature of the circumstances at the time. First, there was the normal large Cabinet, seeking advice from, and working through, the Committee of Imperial Defence. Secondly, there was a large Cabinet assisted by a special body with certain powers of decision, which however would not necessarily be designated a War Committee. Thirdly, there was a large Cabinet delegating wider powers to a smaller body, which in this case would be recognized as a War Committee. Lastly, there was a small War Cabinet, absorbing all the functions of the Cabinet and the Committee of Imperial Defence.

It seemed probable that the first of these arrangements could apply only to a time of full peace. The second might prove effective in a time of crisis or in a minor war. The third would probably be necessary if such a war grew in magnitude or complexity. The fourth alone was likely to suffice in a major war involving the whole of the national effort and the co-operation of Commonwealth nations.

The expedient adopted in 1935, with the Defence Policy Requirements sub-Committee, was thus in accord with the second of these proposals in the appropriate conditions. We have seen the step taken early in 1937 to provide for such a body on a permanent basis. The re-absorption of the subsequent Defence Plans (Policy) sub-Committee within the Committee of Imperial Defence did not invalidate this development, for the former body continued to function as a specific part of the latter. In the spring of 1938, it was provided with means for co-ordinating operations from day to day, which in due course became the Cabinet War Room. But the experience of Munich seemed to require a further step. The prospect of a major war within a year now demanded preparations for a full War Cabinet, whose formation should if possible be approved in principle before war itself broke out. In the course of 1939, it accordingly seemed likely that a small War Cabinet, probably of six or seven Ministers, would come into being on the outbreak of war, with most of its members freed from Departmental duties.

Yet when, on 3 September, a War Cabinet was formed, it was constructed on a somewhat different model. It consisted of nine members—the Prime Minister, the Foreign Secretary, the Chancellor of the Exchequer, the Lord Privy Seal, the Minister for the Co-ordination of Defence, the three Service Ministers, and a Minister without Portfolio—and of these five held Departmental posts. The reasons lay, as usual, in the political and personal circumstances. A Coalition had to be provided for, and there were apparently indispensable personages to be admitted to the inner counsels. The administrative arguments had therefore to be adjusted, as such arguments have always to be adjusted, to the exigencies of the political scene; and indeed Mr Chamberlain may well have felt, as he surveyed his smaller Cabinet with its unusually high proportion of non-Departmental Ministers, that he had reconciled with unusual promptitude and success the demands of his situation with those of the conduct of war.

The War Cabinet functioned reasonably well during its first few months. It did so because the pace of the war was slow. As soon as the Norwegian campaign opened, the defects became apparent. For the system contained a fundamental weakness, deriving—it may be said in retrospect—from a reliance on Lloyd George's type of War Cabinet without an adequate appreciation of the developments which that system was fostering at its close. For in fact, while a small supreme organ seemed necessary to the conduct of a major war, it in turn had, for that very reason, to devolve authority over the different sectors of government; and this process, which had been under way in 1918, had not had time to reach an advanced stage or to strike enduring roots. Different consequences followed in the military and the civil spheres. In the former, the Committee of Imperial Defence developed to meet the needs of rearmament and crisis; but in doing so, lost the active detailed interest of the Prime Minister without replacing his authority by an adequate substitute. In this particular field, hitherto his peculiar province, this was to play Hamlet without the prince; and the peacetime preparations for a small directing body to replace the Cabinet in war thus lacked the essential key. And this key was the more desirable, because the Cabinet had not developed an instrument to direct the civil sector on its behalf, and was in consequence unduly preoccupied with the detail of such affairs. For here the experience of the First World War had not been followed in peace; and indeed one of the most marked characteristics of government in the twenties and thirties was the contrast between the nexus of

Cabinet committees devoted to defence and the absence of such a system in the civil sphere. Successive Cabinets set up plenty of *ad hoc* bodies, as occasion arose. But there were very few permanent central committees at any one time, and only two—the Home Affairs Committee, and the Civil Research Committee, later the Economic Advisory Council—survived throughout the greater part of the period. Their experiences, moreover, were not particularly happy. The standing committees of Cabinet in the First World War had shown a tendency to act as screens for the operations of their sub-committees on the one hand, and for those of their chairmen on the other. The more ambitious of their successors—such as the Economic Advisory Council—showed the same characteristics, while the less ambitious—including the Home Affairs Committee—found themselves limited to the performance of specific functions. When war came again, there was therefore no continuing experience or tradition of a strong central Committee system outside defence and rearmament itself.

These circumstances explain why, in contrast to the Departmental expansion,[1] the War Cabinet confined itself in September 1939 to forming two standing civil committees in addition to the recent Ministerial Priority Committee—the Home Policy Committee (lineal successor to the Home Affairs Committee) and the Civil Defence Committee (first envisaged after the Munich crisis under the title of the Home Security Committee). Others perforce followed within the next few months: an Inter-Departmental Committee of Co-ordination and a

---

[1] See p. 120 above.

Ministerial Committee on Economic Policy, which between them took over many of the functions of the Economic Advisory Council; and a Food Policy sub-Committee, which in April 1940 became an independent Committee of the War Cabinet. The relations between these bodies were not defined with any precision, and fluctuated accordingly. By the spring of 1940, the Committees on Civil Defence and Food Policy had gained ground at the expense of the Home Policy Committee, while the Ministerial Committee on Economic Policy was working in uneasy liaison with the Ministerial Priority Committee formed shortly before the war. The inadequacies of the system increased, as they reflected, those of the War Cabinet itself, and it needed a change in the parent body to simplify and strengthen its subordinates. In the course of 1940 and 1941, the process moved apace. The main standing civil committees were brought under the aegis of a new Lord President of the Council's Committee, which later absorbed the functions of many of the bodies it had been charged to co-ordinate.

This process was the more necessary because from the summer of 1940 the new Prime Minister involved himself once more in the active direction of the military system, and had correspondingly less time to devote to non-military affairs. This welcome change did not arise solely from the fact that the new Prime Minister was Mr Churchill. It was also the result of the unhappy experience of the Minister for the Co-ordination of Defence, and of the Cabinet committee over which he presided. Even in the more leisurely conditions of 'the

phoney war' his position had been awkward. As Lord
Chatfield, the new incumbent of the office, put it—using
almost the very words of the national system that Wolseley had used of the War Office half a century before—he
was 'a fifth wheel to the coach'.[1] It was indeed an
accurate description, for the removal of the Minister
provided an otherwise satisfactory vehicle with adequate
means of propulsion. On the outbreak of war, the extensive organization of the Committee of Imperial Defence
was incorporated immediately in that of the War Cabinet. The Committee itself disappeared, the Chiefs of
Staff sub-Committee became a full Committee of
Cabinet, and the secretariat, reorganized in 1938, was
absorbed in the new Offices of the War Cabinet. In
place of the peacetime Committee, a Ministerial Co-
ordination Committee was established, composed of
the Minister for the Co-ordination of Defence and the
Service Ministers with the Chiefs of Staff as advisers.
But these moves, necessary as they were, were not enough.
Supply had still to be brought into closer touch with
strategy; and, more serious, the organization lacked the
necessary authority. Despite their wide terms of reference, the Ministerial Co-ordination Committee and the
Chiefs of Staff found that the War Cabinet itself was
intervening constantly in their affairs. Deprived of a
working head with adequate power, they could not in
fact remove their operations from the day to day scrutiny
of the supreme body. From April 1940, when the war
took a new turn, the position began to change. The Prime

[1] Admiral of the Fleet Lord Chatfield, *It Might Happen Again*, vol. II
(1947), p. 179. And see p. 18 above.

Minister was forced increasingly to take the chair at meetings of the Ministerial Co-ordination Committee, and the office of Minister for the Co-ordination of Defence was soon allowed to lapse, his place being taken for normal business by the First Lord of the Admiralty. At about the same time, arrangements were made to bring the business of supply regularly before the Committee. But these desirable modifications inevitably suggested the creation of a new organ that would suit them better; and when Mr Churchill replaced Mr Chamberlain as Prime Minister in May, he at once introduced the changes which he had pondered for some time. By combining the office of Prime Minister with that of a new office of Minister of Defence, he brought authority once more where it must lie; and at the same time, he replaced the Ministerial Co-ordination Committee by two Defence Committees, one for operations on which senior Ministers and the Chiefs of Staff sat together, and one, in close association with it, to deal with supply. The anomalies of the rearmament period had now been removed, and the problem of wartime authority reconciled with the peacetime developments in administration.

A new, and splendid, chapter was now about to open. We cannot follow its course here; but we have seen the foundations on which the new achievements were to rise, and which helped to make it possible for the direction of the Second World War, unlike that of the First, to settle into an enduring pattern comparatively early in its course. Three main developments to the Cabinet system may be observed between 1940 and 1945. First, a Prime Minister with exceptional political authority was able to make exceptional use of his professional Service advisers —a process which was supported by the influence of the system in the United States, where the President operated in the military sphere entirely through his Joint Chiefs of Staff. The result was, if I may quote words which I have written elsewhere, 'a silent revolution' in the history of Allied control in war.[1] Supreme control was exercised by a professional and not by a political committee, functioning under the aegis of the Heads of Government. And this innovation marked a further stage in the adjustment of authority, presaged in the First World War, within the British Ministerial system. It saw the disappearance of the Service Ministers from the inner counsels, and their confinement virtually to administrative tasks. In 1922, Lord George Hamilton, recalling the Admiralty as he had known it before the First World War, and reflecting on the First Lord's house, his yacht and his turtle, could write that 'the post. . . is the blue ribbon of offices, and is so recognised by all who have held it'.[2] In 1955, in an important debate in the House of Lords on the organization of defence, several authorities could remark the decline of the Service Ministers from an acknowledged eminence within the Government to a subordinate position on the central committees.

Secondly, Mr Churchill's Administration saw the erection of a powerful and extensive structure of civil committees of Cabinet, comparable with that of the

[1] John Ehrman, *Grand Strategy (vol. VI), October 1944–August 1945* (1956), p. 339.
[2] The Rt Hon. Lord George Hamilton, *Parliamentary Reminiscences and Reflections, 1886–1906* (1922), p. 17.

Committee of Imperial Defence. The growing power of the Lord President's Committee, and the creation of a Production Executive followed by a Ministry of Production, whose Minister supervised a network of central committees in his own sphere, placed at the disposal of the War Cabinet a far more effective and highly articulated hierarchy than had existed before, and one which left its mark on post-war practice.

And thirdly, this devolution of power to the committees drastically altered the conduct of the War Cabinet itself. It was now seldom used as an agent of administration, even at the highest level. It was rather the fountain of administrative development, and a last, exceptional, court of appeal. Cabinet government, bearing its traditional responsibilities to Parliament, never functioned more effectively than during these years of war. But the Cabinet itself, as a body, exercised less direct control of affairs than it had exercised in peace.

It is from the position bequeathed by these last changes that we look back over a period of some fifty years. We do so, as a result, with a sophistication far removed from the attitudes and arguments of those responsible for national defence at its start. But it is a remarkable thing that throughout the immense expansion, and across the experiences of two World Wars, we can recognize a continuous process, and can apply to our problems essentially the same methods of government as those applied half a century ago. The development of the central machinery for defence has in fact taken place in an orderly way. It has thereby helped to preserve, in a revolutionary and warlike age, the essentials of Cabinet government and, it may perhaps be allowed, those of the Parliamentary system within which Cabinet government operates—albeit with powers largely alien to a happier generation. It has been one of the factors that have enabled this country to adjust its economy and its political institutions, without violent interruption, to the burdens of total war, which has been accompanied by such extensive changes to many aspects of the national life.

The path has been cleared by the efforts of a small group of men. Balfour, Haldane, Lloyd George and Churchill among Ministers, Sydenham Clarke, Hankey —above all Hankey—and Ismay among the officials, are the most prominent figures in a process which might well not have emerged or survived without them; and in their histories chance and occasion have played their accustomed parts. But if we isolate these names, it is not to detract from the contributions of others throughout the whole range of government. The central organization at any time is the product of a certain sum of its parts. The value, for instance, of Haldane's contribution to that organization lay perhaps more in his early work at the War Office than his later work for Ramsay Macdonald on the Committee of Imperial Defence itself. And again, to take another instance, Churchill and Ismay could not, in their different capacities, have guided the central mechanism successfully in the Second World War without the intimate support of the individual Chiefs of Staff, representing their Services and in practice their Departments.

But if we must not underrate the contributions of personality and chance, nor must we ignore the effect of the system on the men who ran it. It is sometimes said that good men can make any system work. It seems extremely doubtful; and in any case good men, placed in such a position, have usually done their best to see that the system is changed. At best, an inadequate organization cramps and disturbs the efforts of those who have to run it: at the worst, it nullifies them. The members of Lloyd George's War Cabinet were probably men of higher calibre than those of Mr Churchill's. But the Cabinet system worked far better in the second case than in the first. And who can say what Kitchener might not have done within a more effective system of control, or deny that his peculiar activities would have been impossible in the Second World War? This, of course, is not to exaggerate the impact of machinery upon events. When fundamental disagreements arise, or there is a fundamental lack of harmony, nothing can disguise the fact, or do more than mitigate the consequences. It is, moreover, a common experience for wrong decisions to be taken in the right way, and for the best preparations and organization to be rendered powerless by circumstances beyond control. But such facts increase, rather than diminish, the importance of their native system to the men who have to face them. The comparative excellence of the Chiefs of Staff and the higher commanders in the Second World War must have owed a great deal to the experience and atmosphere in which they were trained, the result of an increased familiarity with the institutions through which they had to work and an increased awareness of the principles informing them. The higher elements in the Services had been brought again, from their isolation in the nineteenth century, into the structure and habits of British administration. And this achievement was itself part of a more extensive, and a notable, process: the reincorporation of one of the three classic activities of government, after a long period of virtual disuse, into the framework and traditions of government as a whole.

INDEX

Admiralty, 6, 8, 18–20, 22, 30, 38, 40–1, 45–8, 58–9, 64, 66, 70–1, 84–5, 101, 128
  See also Deputy First Sea Lord; Director of Mobilization; Director of Naval Intelligence; First Lord of the Admiralty; First Sea Lord; Naval Staff
  Assistant Secretary of, 46
  War Council, 46
Aerial Operations Committee, 75
Agadir crisis, 47
Agriculture, Board of, 71
Air, Secretary of State for, 102, 105, 122, 126, 128
  See also Churchill, Winston S.
Air Boards, 102
Air Committee, 43
Air Council, 102, 103
Air Ministry, 96, 102
  See also Air Council, Air Staff
Air Organization Committee, 102
Air Policy Committee, 102
Air Staff, 103–4
  See also Portal of Hungerford
Algeciras Conference, 36
Allied Naval Council, 94
Allied Transportation Council, 94
Anglo-Japanese Treaty (1905), 29
Armaments Output Committee, 64–5
Army and Navy Pay Committee, 97
Army Board, 18
Army Council, 32, 34, 36, 58, 82, 101
Arnold-Foster, H. O., 24, 28–9, 32, 33, 34
Asquith, H. H., 27–8, 49, 50, 54, 57, 67, 69, 76–7, 78, 87

Baldwin, Stanley, 112, 118–19

Balfour, A. J., 13, 28–30, 31, 50, 55, 59, 76, 85, 96, 107, 109, 119, 130
Barnes, George, 72 n.
Beresford Enquiry, 46
Bermuda, 10
Blockade, Ministry of, 69
'Blue-water' school, the, 27, 37, 38, 103
British Expeditionary Force, 38–9, 41, 47, 55, 60
British Military Representative, Versailles, 92–3
  See also Rawlinson, Sir Henry; Sackville-West, Hon. Charles
Brodrick, St John, 27

Cabinet. *See* Imperial War Cabinet; War Cabinet
Cabinet, War Committees, 56–8, 67, 76, 78–9, 80, 121
  See also Committee of Imperial Defence, Dardanelles Committee, Offensive sub-Committee, War Committee, War Council
Cabinet Committee on Munitions, 64
Cabinet War Room, 122
Campbell-Bannerman, Sir Henry, 17, 35, 41
Carnarvon, 4th Earl of, 9
Carson, Sir Edward, 72 n., 84
Chamberlain, Austen, 72 n.
Chamberlain, Joseph, 15
Chamberlain, Neville, 78, 79, 81, 122, 127
Chanak crisis, 109
Chatfield, Lord, 126
Chiefs of Staff, 81, 87, 104, 109–10, 112, 113, 117, 126, 127–8, 130, 131
  Committee, 109–10, 119, 126